OUR FIVE SE...

Touch

Sally Morgan

WAYLAND

Explore the world with **Popcorn** - your complete first non-fiction library.

Look out for more titles in the **Popcorn** range. All books have the same format of simple text and awesome images. Text is carefully matched to the pictures to help readers to identify and understand key vocabulary. www.waylandbooks.co.uk/popcorn

First published in 2009 by Wayland
Copyright Wayland 2009

Wayland
Hachette Children's Books
338 Euston Road
London NW1 3BH

Wayland Australia
Level 17/207 Kent Street
Sydney NSW 2000

Editor: Nicola Edwards
Designer: Robert Walster
Picture researcher: Shelley Noronha
Series consultant: Kate Ruttle
Design concept: Paul Cherrill

British Library Cataloguing in Publication Data
Morgan, Sally
Touch. - (Popcorn. Five senses)
1. Touch - Juvenile literature
I. Title
612.8'8
ISBN: 978 0 7502 5768 8

Printed and bound in China

Wayland is a division of Hachette Children's Books,
an Hachette UK Company
www.hachette.co.uk

Photographs:
Cover Nicole S Young/istock; title page
Patrick Oberem/istock; p2 Rob Cruse/istock;
p4 Bananastock / Jupiter Images / ImagePick;
p5 Aldo Murillo/istock; p6 Katrina
Brown/Shutterstock; p7 Lindqvist/istock; p8
Martyn f. Chillmaid; p9 Stacy Barnett/istock;
p10 Nicole S Young/istock; p11 Peter Cairns/
Ecoscene; p12 Benjamin Howell/Shutterstock;
p13 © Tim Pannell/Corbis; p14 ©
Wolf/zefa/Corbis; p15 © Ned Frisk/Corbis;
p16 © Roy McMahon/Corbis; p18 Patrick
Oberem/istock; p19 Rob Cruse/istock; © Todd
Pusser/naturepl.com; p21 Michael
Gore/Ecoscene; p22 (both) Martyn f.
Chillmaid; p23 Martyn f. Chillmaid

Contents

Touch

Every day we touch many different things, such as the clothes that we wear and the food that we eat.

When we tie our shoelaces we touch them with our fingers.

Touch is one of our five senses. We touch things to find out about our surroundings. Touch protects us, too.

Touching someone we love can make us feel happy.

Our five senses are sight, hearing, touch, smell and taste.

Our skin

We touch using our skin, from our face to our fingertips to our toes. Hairs grow from the skin. These hairs help us to feel things, too.

We can feel with every part of the skin that covers our bodies.

Thick skin covers the soles of our feet. Thin skin covers our eyelids. The skin on our arms and legs is smooth but it is wrinkled on our elbows and knees.

Loose skin covers our knees so that we can bend our legs.

Touch and the skin

When we touch something, special detectors in the skin send messages to the brain. The detectors can feel hot and cold, pressure and pain.

Blind people read Braille using their sense of touch.

Braille is a system of tiny raised dots that spell out words.

The skin on our fingertips, lips, and the back of our neck is very sensitive to touch. The thick soles of our feet feel very little.

Rashes make our skin feel itchy.

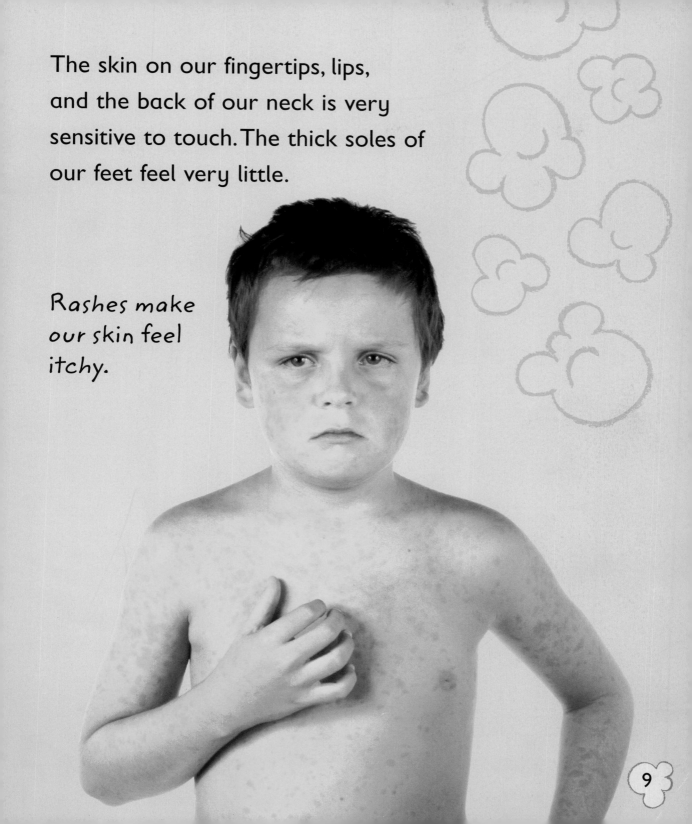

Textures

When you run your fingertips over the surface of an object you feel its texture. Feel the cover of this book. It has a smooth, slippery surface.

Sand has a gritty and rough texture.

We use many different words to describe texture. Textures can be rough or smooth, bumpy or squidgy, prickly or fluffy.

What textures would you feel if you were walking through this wood?

Can you think of any other words for textures?

✋ Hot or cold?

Our skin can feel if something is hot or cold. For example, a melting ice cube feels cold when we touch it. A towel from the airing cupboard feels warm.

Touching food with our lips and tongue tells us if it is hot or cold.

In cold weather we cover our skin with warm clothes. In hot weather, we wear thin, light clothing so that our skin does not get too hot.

Our skin can tell the difference between a warm breeze and a cold wind.

Warning touch

Our sense of touch helps to protect us from danger. When we touch a hot object, our skin feels the heat. We do not have to think about how to react. Instantly we pull our finger away.

Ouch! Touching the sharp spines of a cactus can be painful.

These instant reactions are called reflexes. We cannot control a reflex. It happens without our brain being involved.

Kitchens can be dangerous places and our reflexes protect us from harm.

Protecting the skin

Skin can be damaged by sunlight. Our skin burns if we stay in the sun for too long. Sunburned skin feels very painful. We can protect our skin by covering it with suncream.

If you are playing in the sun, use suncream to protect your skin.

Cold weather can harm our skin, especially the skin on our fingers and toes. In extreme cold, unprotected fingers and toes may freeze and feel numb.

In cold weather we protect our skin by wearing thick gloves and shoes.

If our skin is harmed, our sense of touch works less well.

Using touch

We use our sense of touch to find out information about our surroundings. Imagine walking barefoot along a path with your eyes closed. Your sense of touch would tell you if the ground was wet, or bumpy or slippery.

Babies use touch to explore their world.

We use touch when we pick up objects, hold cutlery at meal times and play musical instruments. Our fingers help us to play with toys and use a computer keyboard.

We use our sense of touch to plant seeds and seedlings, to pick fruit and pull up vegetables.

Animals and touch

Many animals use touch to locate food or to find their way around. Touch is very important to animals that have poor eyesight, such as moles and elephants.

The star-nosed mole has tentacles around its nose that it uses to touch.

Animals use their sense of touch when they look after their young. Some animals use their fingers to keep their fur clean. This is called grooming.

This monkey is picking off dirt and fleas from the fur of another monkey.

21

Your sense of touch

See if you can identify objects just by touch. Put the objects you've collected in a deep box.

You will need:
• a deep box • a glove
• small objects such as an apple, a piece of foil, a sponge, a bar of soap, a small battery, a leaf and a feather.

Look away and put your hand in the box. Pick up one of the objects, keeping your hand in the box. Can you tell which object it is just by using your sense of touch? Do this for all the objects. Try to describe the texture of each one.

Now try the activity again but this time wearing the glove. Is it more difficult to identify the objects? Why do you think this is?

22

Sensitive skin

Some parts of your skin are more sensitive than others. Ask a friend to help you try this test. Hold two pencils together. Ask your friend to touch the tips of both pencils gently on the skin of your palm, forearm, and upper arm.

Each time, tell your friend whether you can feel both tips or just one. Where the skin is very sensitive, you should feel two tips. Where it is less sensitive you may feel only one.

Glossary

Braille writing made up of small, raised dots that blind people can read

brain the control centre of the body, found inside the head

detectors structures in the skin that pick up signals, such as pain, pressure, heat and cold

numb without feeling

pressure force pushing or pressing down on something, for example pressing on a button

rashes itchy red patches of skin

reflex an instant reaction

sensitive able to detect or feel something

Index

LIFE WORLD LIBRARY
CHINA

LIFE WORLD LIBRARY

CHINA

by Loren Fessler
and The Editors of LIFE

TIME-LIFE INTERNATIONAL (Nederland) N.V.

COVER: Construction workers taking
part in the dedication of the
Ming Tombs dam outside Peking in 1958,
assemble on the sun-drenched hillside
to watch the festivities.

ABOUT THE WRITER

Loren Fessler, the author of the interpretive text for this volume of the
LIFE World Library, has made a speciality of Chinese history, literature and
politics ever since he was sent to China by the U.S. Army's Office of Strategic
Services during World War II. There he served with Nationalist Chinese
paratroops. In 1948-9 he interrupted his studies at Harvard to enrol at
Lingnan University in Canton, China, and later spent two years studying
Chinese language and literature at the University of Washington. A TIME-
LIFE correspondent on Taiwan for four years, he was a member of the
company's Hong Kong Bureau from 1958 until 1966, when he returned to
Harvard to continue his studies of Chinese affairs at the University's East
Asian Research Center.

The British crown colony of Hong Kong is the West's primary listening
post for information on Red China, which does not grant entry visas to
many foreigners. There, with other Western journalists, the consular officials from a dozen nations and other sinologists, Mr. Fessler performed
the difficult detective work of trying to follow what was happening on the
mainland of China. He examined the Chinese publications that reach
Hong Kong and kept in touch with the several agencies that monitor
Chinese radio broadcasts. He interviewed refugees from China, obtained
information from United States government agencies that report on the
mainland, consulted foreign diplomats and businessmen who travel in
China and sought the opinion of China specialists at Hong Kong University. From these and many other sources he has pieced together the com-
prehensive picture of life in China today contained in this present volume.

Contents

TIME/LIFE BOOKS

EDITOR

Maitland A. Edey

TEXT DIRECTOR   ART DIRECTOR

Jerry Korn   *Edward A. Hamilton*

CHIEF OF RESEARCH

Beatrice T. Dobie

EDITORIAL STAFF FOR "CHINA"

EDITOR, LIFE WORLD LIBRARY   *Oliver E. Allen*

DESIGNER   *Ben Schultz*

CHIEF RESEARCHER   *Grace Brynolson*

The text for this book was written by Loren Fessler, the picture essays by David S. Thomson and Edmund V. White. Valuable help in preparing the book was provided by the following individuals and departments of Time Inc.: James Burke, John Dominis, Dmitri Kessel and Howard Sochurek, LIFE staff photographers; Doris O'Neil, Chief, LIFE Picture Library; Peter Draz, Chief of the Bureau of Editorial Reference; Richard M. Clurman, Chief, TIME-LIFE News Service; and Jerrold Schecter and Wong Bing Wong of the Hong Kong Bureau. This international edition adapted by Laura Ford.

Preface

An informed public is essential for the development of sound foreign policies. We owe it to ourselves to know as much as we possibly can about our contemporary world. And who can deny that China is a most important part of that world? When one in every five occupants of our globe is Chinese, it would seem the most obvious kind of self-interest to know as much as we can about them and about the many forces that have shaped and influenced them throughout their long history. An ambitious and aggressive Communist China represents a serious threat to us and to all of its neighbours. But we can never hope to meet that threat successfully, or to encourage developments favourable to world stability or to our own interests, if we shut our eyes and close our minds.

When the Communists won control over the mainland in 1949, there ensued a heated but largely fruitless debate here on the question "Who lost China?" Many Americans wrote off Communist China as a huge but willing puppet of Moscow. Now that cliché has been shattered on the rocks of the deepening Sino-Soviet rift. One can imagine another "Who lost China?" debate going on today—this time in the Kremlin. The fact is, of course, that China was not ours or the Russians' to lose. The victorious and vanquished are the Chinese themselves. And if the history of that troubled land suggests anything, it is that the struggle among internal forces will continue.

There are encouraging signs that Americans are now seeking a deeper understanding of the facts of life as they pertain to China, past and present. In doing so, we need not—indeed, should not—confuse awareness for approval. There is a vast difference between recognizing facts and approving policies and actions. The author quotes an ancient Chinese maxim: *Know your opponents; know yourself.*

This book is a good example of our re-awakening interest in Chinese history and current developments. Our great universities and research centres are devoting increasing time and energy to study and analysis. Translations of Chinese Communist materials undertaken by the United States government are the backbone of much of the private and official investigation of the Chinese Communists.

Fortunately, we are not cut off entirely from the Chinese people, whose friendship we have sought since the days of the clipper ships. We enjoy cordial and rewarding relations with the government of the Republic of China now on Taiwan, which we recognize as the legitimate government of China. We have important contacts, too, with millions of Chinese in Hong Kong, Malaysia and elsewhere.

As for the Chinese on the mainland, no one can predict when their isolation will end. But their separation from their neighbours and from all free peoples is such an obvious tragedy that we must hope that it is only a temporary phenomenon.

Meantime, we can better understand modern China and how it reached its present condition by drawing on the scholarship and experience of men like Loren Fessler. The Editors of the LIFE World Library have done us all a service by making available this readable and thoughtful review of the history of a great but tragically exploited people.

Surely all Americans must look forward to the day when these talented people with their rich culture are reunited with us and with the rest of the world in friendship, co-operation and freedom, when we are working together towards the goal President John F. Kennedy once described as ". . . a peaceful community of free and independent states, free to choose their own future and their own system, so long as it does not threaten the freedom of others".

W. AVERELL HARRIMAN
U.S. Under Secretary of State
for Political Affairs

Sightseers stroll through the Forbidden city in Peking. Once the official residence of emperors, the palace was out of bounds to all but

the highest officials for centuries. Now it is open to the public.

1

An Immense and Crowded Land

CHINA is an ancient land of superlatives. Its western mountains, soaring to heights of 24,000 feet and more, share with the Himalayas the distinction of being the world's tallest; in the North-West, China possesses one of the lowest spots on earth, the Turfan Depression, which lies 505 feet below sea-level. For 1,500 miles across the country's northern provinces winds the longest structure ever made by man, the Great Wall, erected more than 2,000 years ago to slow the encroachments of peoples from the steppes of Asia. In area, China is exceeded only by Canada and the Soviet Union, and it has by far the largest population in the world—considerably more than 700 million people. Behind that statistic lies the country's most overwhelming problem and its greatest challenge, for the most important fact about China is that it does not have sufficient superlatives. It lacks enough cultivable land to feed its constantly increasing numbers. Already so numerous are the people of this giant nation that at least one out of every five persons on earth is Chinese.

There is no sameness about them or their land. Chinese cities and towns are jammed with workers and bureaucrats, and on crowded plains and in river valleys peasants work elbow to elbow. Yet China has two million square miles where camel caravans and survey teams can travel for days and meet not a single soul. In the frost-stunted birch forests on the Siberian border, sturdy, windburned mountain men trap beaver and pan for gold. In the great industrial centre of Shanghai, pale-faced clerks nervously calculate production figures on abaci built to designs centuries old. In the jungle of Hainan Island, close to the south coast of the mainland, aboriginal Li tribesmen work on road and timber projects, supervised by young cadres sent out from the northern cities. In the vastness of the autonomous region of Sinkiang, a North-West area three times the size of France, tough Uighur horsemen watch sullenly as dust-covered trucks arrive packed with "pioneers" from the crowded coastal cities.

The Chinese are a clannish people, highly sensitive to the differences of strangers from other villages and provinces, and frequently unflattering in their judgments about outsiders. Northern Chinese regard themselves as even-tempered, cultured and shrewdly conservative; they consider southerners to be quick-tempered, crude and unreliably revolutionary. Southerners, on the other hand, regard themselves as sensibly progressive and northern Chinese as wilfully old-fashioned. Everyone has complaints about the Shanghainese; they are city slickers with no culture. Men from Hunan province are believed to make the best generals;

men from land-poor Chekiang province, skilled as bandits and pirates, are regarded as the best mercenaries. The coastal Fukienese are stereotyped as stingy *san pa tao*, or "three blades", good only for the three blade-wielding crafts of cooking, barbering and tailoring. Stereotypes aside, the land is so vast and communications have so long been primitive that the differences among the peoples of China can be very real.

Contributing to the differences is the country's troublesome language problem. All literate Chinese, regardless of their home provinces, read and write the same language. But literate Chinese are a minority. Perhaps 400 million out of the 700 million people speak or understand a variety of *Kuo-yu*, or Mandarin, the "national" tongue. But another 300 million rely on an assortment of languages and dialects so numerous that not all have been tallied.

It is the land itself, however, that remains the over-riding problem. China is a far harsher country than either the Soviet Union or Canada, and it has three times as many people to feed as those two larger nations combined.

The western two thirds of China bulges up in high, dry plateaux and a mass of towering mountain ranges. A number of north-south ranges further reduce China's arable land in the east. In all, only 10 to 15 per cent of the total land area can now be used for farming; the rest is too steep, too dry, too high or too exhausted.

Most of the land that can be cultivated lies in the eastern third of China, in the plains and in the areas drained by the great rivers—the Amur, the Yellow, the Yangtze and the West. In this eastern third live about 90 per cent of the country's inhabitants. The western two

ONE COUNTRY, TWO GOVERNMENTS

This volume concerns itself with China as a whole, an area which in effect has two governments. In Peking, on the mainland, is the Communist government of the People's Republic of China, whose political leader is Mao Tse-tung. Off the mainland on the island of Taiwan is the Nationalist government (so called because it is run by the Kuomintang or National People's party) of what is officially known as the Republic of China, led by Chiang Kai-shek. The Communists have since 1949 held control of the mainland (more than 700 million people in 3.8 million square miles), while the Nationalists rule some 13 million people on 14,000 square miles, including Taiwan, the near-by Pescadores and the islands of Quemoy and Matsu. But both Mao Tse-tung and Chiang Kai-shek, while challenging each other's authority, use the term "China" to include the mainland and Taiwan thirds is China's giant-sized version of the American West of a century ago. A forbidding region of permanently snow-capped mountains looming over arid valleys, the west is the home of most of the peoples that China classifies as "national minorities"—the Tibetans, Uighurs, Kazakhs, Miao, Yi and Mongols, who for long have lived on the periphery of Chinese civilization. These people could be called China's Indians. Treated like the tribes American empire builders pushed aside in their march to the U.S. West, these minorities have for centuries resisted Chinese encroachment.

But in China now, as in 19th-century America, the pioneers outgun the tribes. They have behind them the power of a determined government that is pressed for food and industrial raw materials. Every year hundreds of thousands of Chinese are sent to the west. Eventually they will outnumber the minorities, for this frontier is the hope of China. Here, in Sinkiang and the province of Chinghai, labour battalions and commune workers are attempting to reclaim the arid grasslands, linking them by extensive irrigation ducts to the water of the glaciated hills. This is a key region in Communist planners' dreams of doubling the country's arable area.

During the last century Chinese leaders have nevertheless grown painfully aware that nations do not become powerful on agriculture alone. In their still incompletely surveyed west, the Chinese hope to expand their industrial potential, as well as to increase their supplies of grain, cotton and wool. Near Yumen (Jade Gate), at the western terminus of the Great Wall in Kansu province, a sprawling refinery has been built. It processes crude oil from the fields straddling the Kansu-Chinghai border.

POPULATION: AN ESTIMATE

No one knows precisely how many people live within the borders of China, for Chinese censuses have for long been notoriously inaccurate. The last Chinese Nationalist census, taken in 1947, put the population at 463 million; the last Chinese Communist census, in 1953, fixed it at 582 million. The Chinese Nationalists claim that this figure was far too high. The United States Census Bureau, on the other hand, believes that the count was too low, and many Western experts agree. Yet the 1953 census was probably the most accurate count ever made of the Chinese. Since it was taken, experts estimate that the country's population has been increasing at an annual rate of at least 2 to 2.2 per cent. The best guess, therefore, is that China had between 753 and 775 million people in 1966, and that the population will reach the thousand million mark by 1980.

Along the railway connecting Kansu and Sinkiang with eastern China the Communists are building iron and steel plants. Elsewhere in the region civilian settlers and army units work deposits of coal, iron, lead, sulphur, gold and uranium.

In this area China is testing thermonuclear weapons and working on ballistic missiles. Much of what goes on here, especially around Lop Nor and an old oasis town named Chiuchuan (Liquor Springs), is known only to a few select planners—and perhaps to distant specialists who evaluate data from Tiroslike satellites and monitoring devices borne by American-built U-2s flown from Taiwan. Named Formosa by the Portuguese in the 16th century, this 13,808-square-mile island, 100 miles off the southeastern coast of China, has been the seat of the Nationalist government since the Chinese Communists took over the mainland in 1949.

Although developments in the west may some day remake the face of China, the country's eastern third remains its most important area. Here grow most of China's crops. Here is the bulk of the industrial plant. This is the heartland.

Eastern China consists of four major regions: (1) the North-East, (2) the Lower Yellow River region, (3) the Yangtze River drainage area and (4) South China.

The first region is known to outsiders as Manchuria. Before World War II the Japanese named it Manchukuo, but the Chinese have long referred to it as *Tung-pei*, the North-East. It has a cold, dry climate resembling that of the praries of western Canada. The region's topography—mountains giving way to rolling plains which rise into mountains—is vaguely like that of

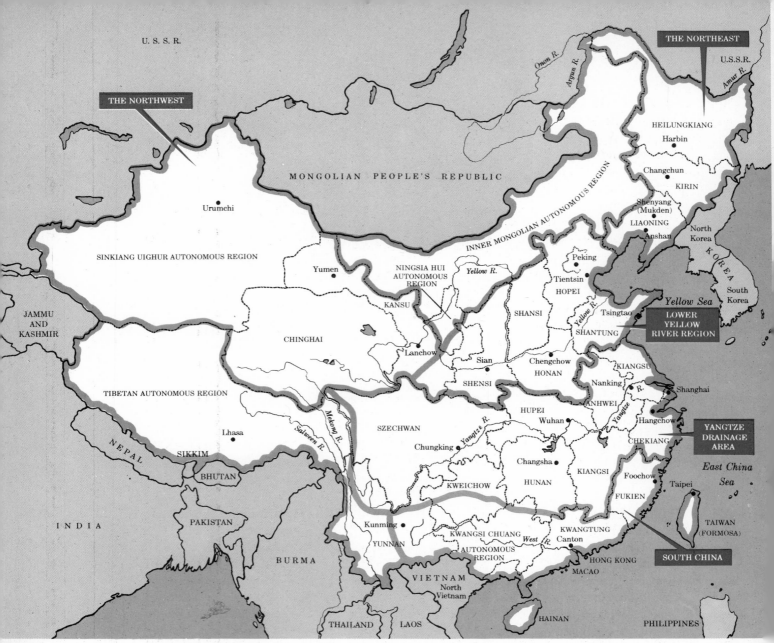

U.S.S.R.

THE NORTHEAST

THE NORTHWEST

U.S.S.R.

Onon R. *Argun R.* *Amur R.*

MONGOLIAN PEOPLE'S REPUBLIC

HEILUNGKIANG

Harbin

Changchun

KIRIN

Urumchi

INNER MONGOLIAN AUTONOMOUS REGION

Shenyang
(Mukden)

LIAONING

North
Korea

Anshan

SINKIANG UIGHUR AUTONOMOUS REGION

Yumen

NINGSIA HUI
AUTONOMOUS
REGION

Yellow R.

Peking

Tientsin

HOPEI

KOREA

KANSU

SHANSI

Yellow R.

Tsingtao

LOWER
YELLOW
RIVER REGION

South
Korea

Yellow Sea

CHINGHAI

Lanchow

SHANTUNG

JAMMU
AND
KASHMIR

Sian

Chengchow

HONAN

KIANGSU

Nanking

R.

Shanghai

SHENSI

ANHWEI

Yangtze

TIBETAN AUTONOMOUS REGION

HUPEI

Wuhan

Hangchow

Mekong R.

Salween R.

SZECHWAN

Yangtze R.

CHEKIANG

YANGTZE
DRAINAGE
AREA

Lhasa

Chungking

Changsha

KIANGSI

*East China
Sea*

NEPAL

SIKKIM

HUNAN

Foochow

Taipei

KWEICHOW

FUKIEN

BHUTAN

INDIA

PAKISTAN

Kunming

KWANGSI CHUANG

KWANGTUNG

TAIWAN
(FORMOSA)

YUNNAN

West R.

Canton

AUTONOMOUS
REGION

SOUTH CHINA

BURMA

HONG KONG

MACAO

VIETNAM

North
Vietnam

HAINAN

PHILIPPINES

THAILAND

LAOS

PRINCIPAL GEOGRAPHICAL AREAS of China, as described in this chapter, are outlined in colour above. Provincial boundaries are in black; some provinces extend into two regions.

The Mongolian People's Republic is an independent nation between China and the U.S.S.R., whereas the Inner Mongolian Autonomous Region is an administrative subdivision of China.

the United States. From the wooded foothills of the Changpai Mountains in the east comes much of the coal and iron for the region's industries. From dams on the Yalu River comes electric power for both North Korea and China, while oil from the new Taching fields supplies much of China's needs. In the centre of the North-East lies China's biggest and most fertile plain, roughly 140,000 square miles of gently rolling loam and clay. Here, huge, mechanized state farms produce sugar beets, soya beans,

wheat and other crops important to the economy.

The North-East has been a much coveted land. Chinese, Russian and Japanese rivalries in the region date back to the late 19th century. Chronic famine in the near-by provinces of Shantung and Hopei periodically drove floods of Chinese into the North-East. Until World War II, however, the Russians and the Japanese, who began building railways and industries in the area at the turn of the century, dominated the economy and politics of the

North-East. The Soviets moved into the Japanese-held areas of the North-East a week before the end of World War II and removed or destroyed Japanese industrial equipment worth between £285 million and £715 million. Later, they felt compelled to help the Chinese Communists to rebuild the region. With a population of perhaps 60 million, the area now produces a third of China's coal, steel and machine tools, and most of its railway stock.

THE second region of eastern China, the Lower Yellow River area, is rightly called the cradle of Chinese civilization by anthropologists and archaeologists. The capitals of the earliest of China's great dynasties were situated here, and the Communists have seen fit to restore Peking as the capital of modern China. But the Lower Yellow River valley, for all its distinguished history, has for long been a region plagued with misery. Nowhere else in China is the struggle of the Chinese to master nature more bitter and apparent.

In the semi-arid Yellow River provinces of Kansu, Honan, Shansi and Shensi, millions of people live in caves hollowed out of the incalculable tons of wind-blown silt called loess which have been deposited over thousands of years on the region's hillsides. In the flatter areas to the east, peasants make their homes in small huts constructed of pounded earth, mud-plastered wattle or poorly fired clay bricks. So intensely settled is the limited land that the earth-coloured villages, surrounded by ancestral graves and fields of grain and cotton, seldom lie out of sight of neighbouring villages.

For thousands of years the region has undergone a tragic cycle of famine and flood. Century after century the silt-laden Yellow River, "China's Sorrow", has gradually built up its bed, and year after year hundreds of thousands of peasants have patiently toiled along the river's banks, raising dykes to contain its overflow. In many places the flood surface of the river rises 25 feet above the plains. When flood waters breach the dykes, disaster follows. Tens of thousands of square miles of cropland are submerged. Walled towns sandbag their gates and become islands in a great brown sea flecked with bloated bodies and rotting grain. At other times drought scourges the region; the dry earth cracks and the crops shrivel. Brutalizing famine conditions, forcing many people to sell their children into servitude and driving others to cannibalism, have periodically cursed this section of China for more than 2,000 years.

To the south of the Yellow River lies the third region of the Chinese heartland, the area drained by the Yangtze. The Yangtze valley area encompasses some 435,000 square miles of the heartland and holds some 350 million people—more than the entire populations of the Soviet Union, Great Britain and France combined.

THE cities in this region—Shanghai, Nanking and Chungking—are closely associated with the drama of recent Chinese history. Shanghai, once an undistinguished trading town on the mud-flats near the mouth of the Yangtze, was opened as a treaty port in 1843. By 1850 opium constituted 54 per cent of the city's import trade, and by 1870 more than 60 per cent of China's exports and imports were moving through the port. Shanghai's reputation as a centre of sin and sharp practice soon became world wide; the verb "to shanghai" became part of every seaman's vocabulary. The Communists have succeeded to an extent in toning down the old city. Free enterprise in sin and industry has largely disappeared. But Shanghai is still the country's biggest textile centre and, with its satellite towns, numbers a population of more than 10 million.

Nanking, 200 miles up the Yangtze, is best known as the pre-war seat of Chiang Kai-shek's Nationalist government, which abandoned the city just before its capture and sacking by the Japanese in 1937. Once a capital of imperial China, it had known violence before. In 1853 the T'ai P'ing rebels, who combined a bizarre form of Christianity with 19th-century proletarian reform aspirations, stormed the city. They held it as their capital until imperial troops retook the gutted city in 1864. Nanking today is quiet and provincial, although the Communists claim that it is becoming a centre of light industry.

Still farther up-river, protected deep in the interior of the province of Szechwan by tortuous mountain passes and the turbulent Yangtze gorges, is Chungking, Nationalist China's wartime capital for more than eight years. Western diplomats and uprooted Chinese alike cursed Chungking's damp climate, muggy in summer and raw in winter. But the humidity helps to give the Red Basin that lies to the north of Chungking an 11-month growing season, and it was the Red Basin which fed Chiang's refugee government.

CHUNGKING remains an important shipping and trading centre for the food grown in the Red Basin, so named from the brick-red sandstone which colours its productive plains. From the plains, where an ingenious irrigation system has prevented flooding for more than 2,000 years, come rice, wheat, sugar cane and cotton. From the foothills of the mountains that encircle the plains, and from terraces carved 50 tiers high into their flanks, come sweet potatoes, rice, barley, millet and peas. In the old days opium, too, was grown here. On the banks of the terraces and on the ridge lines, tung, mulberry and citrus trees vie for space with tea plants. In the land itself lie reserves of salt, coal and iron.

An area less generously endowed by nature than Szechwan and the rest of the Yangtze valley is the fourth region of the Chinese heartland, that dominated by the West River in South China. Economically the poorest of the four regions, South China has for long bred innovators, agitators and trouble.

Western seekers of empire got their first foothold in China in the south, at Macao and Canton. Clashes between Western forces and Chinese authorities opposed to the entry of opium into China took place in the waters south of Canton and led to China's loss of Hong Kong to Britain in 1842. Sun Yat-sen, a

Cantonese educated in Hong Kong and Honolulu, returned to the city and became in the 1890s the leader of the revolutionary movement that overthrew the Manchu Dynasty in 1911 and established the first Chinese Republic. In Canton in later years a young officer named Chiang Kai-shek worked with other obscure firebrands like Mao Tse-tung and Chou En-lai.

Cantonese tend to be shorter in build and more aggressive than northerners. On the rocky, gently rolling hills of their semi-tropical region they raise rice, sweet potatoes and tea. But they are by no means wealthy. So limited is the cultivable land in fact that, despite imperial regulations against emigration, the Cantonese and their Fukienese neighbours to the north-east were for centuries the greatest emigrants in Asia. They pushed overseas to Taiwan, the Philippines, South-East Asia and the Americas, remaining essentially Chinese but constantly exposing themselves to new and unorthodox ideas.

Letters and visits from these emigrants influenced their stay-at-home relatives, often making them restive and dissatisfied. To this day Chinese Communist officials worry about "bourgeois" influences entering the region through continuing contacts with the overseas Chinese and the foreign settlements at Hong Kong and Macao.

South China is not the only area where there is restiveness and dissatisfaction. One of the worries of the Communists is what they call the "spontaneous tendency towards capitalism" in rural areas throughout the country, a tendency again reflecting the basic Chinese problem—the shortage of arable land.

The proper ratio of man to land has been of continuing concern in China for thousands of years. More than 200 years before the birth of Christ, a philosopher named Han Fei Tzu contrasted the "ancient times" when people were few to the conditions of his own day: "People at present think five children are not excessive, and families have five children. Thus there are more people and wealth is less; toil has become hard and provisions meagre."

Chinese society has experienced numerous flowerings since Han Fei Tzu's day, but the toil has increased and the provisions have become scantier, for the man-to-land problem has remained and intensified. At various times famines, plagues, wars or migrations to other areas in China have relieved the pressure. But in recent years migration has not offered a way out; through the centuries China's cultivable areas have filled up, and the Chinese peasant has been forced to adapt himself to the ever more grinding task of forcing every possible bit of food out of every bit of land he can lay his hands on.

Village life in China by any standard is a constant struggle for physical survival—a survival of the strongest, the shrewdest and, often, the most hardhearted. By Western standards peasant life is so harsh as to seem hardly worth living. But it is this struggle and this poverty which have made the Chinese peasants, and indeed the Chinese people at large, what they are today. Inured to hardship, cynical of promises, accustomed to discipline, they have become experts at survival.

England used to be called a nation of shopkeepers. China can be called a nation of peasants. Although its cities flow with people, eight out of 10 of its citizens live in a million tiny farming villages. These villages, most of them spread from the dusty wheat fields south of

---

LANGUAGE: TONES AND DIALECTS

Chinese is a tonal language which consists of words that are generally one syllable long. Tone is as important in determining meaning as consonants and vowels. For example, one syllable uttered on four different tones can mean four different things.

The hundreds of Chinese dialects differ so much that the speaker of one often cannot understand the speaker of another. For instance, the word for "no" is pronounced "bu" in Mandarin, the dialect of Peking, and "baht" in Cantonese.

Most Chinese names in this book are transliterated in the familiar Wade-Giles system, the best known of many. No attempt to render tones is made. All *a*'s are said like the *a* in "father". If *ch, k, p* and *t* are not followed by an apostrophe, pronounce their sounds as *j, g, b* and *d*. The name of China's Premier, Chou En-lai, is pronounced "Joe Un-lye".

Peking to the sub-tropical valleys around Canton, tend to share the common denominators of antiquity, poverty and primitiveness.

Most of the villages have no motor-road link with each other or with the rest of the country. In 1943 China had less than 80,000 miles of roads. Today the Communists claim 300,000 miles. This is barely 8 per cent of the 3.6 million miles in the United States, whose land area is only some 10 per cent less than that of China. Rural transport still depends primarily on cart tracks and footpaths. Such modern vehicles as wheelbarrows fitted with rubber tyres or ball bearings are greatly in demand.

Electricity is still a showpiece rarity in the villages. Candles and oil lamps are too expensive for most villagers; when the sun goes down the peasants go to bed. Few can read; most are ignorant of the outside world. Almost all have heard of the Communist party Chairman Mao Tse-tung, but many cannot identify two such important men in Communist China as the Premier of the People's Republic, Chou En-lai, or the Defence Minister, Lin Piao. Many peasants have no idea of the name of the governor of their province or of the head of their commune—and they do not care.

P EASANT farming methods vary with the locality, but they are everywhere primitive. Only in pilot projects in the North-East and in the North-West is mechanization much more than a dream. The peasants must rely on water buffalo or donkeys for heavy ploughing. Even then the planting, transplanting, weeding, fertilizing, harvesting and reaping must be done by hand. Working a tiny plot of ground, aided by a hoe and the human fertilizer called "night soil", the Chinese peasant produces only enough to feed himself and two other people. Even a relatively prosperous peasant family exists on a level barely above subsistence, and one bit of misfortune can push such a family over the brink, down to the poor-peasant status of perpetual want, hunger and debt.

Under such circumstances, the thought uppermost in every village family's mind is: how

can we get more land, and thus more food and income? The question is virtually insoluble. There is little land for anyone to get.

Communist China may now have 270 million acres of arable land. Just a little less than half an acre is available to each of the approximately 580 million members of peasant families. In South China, where crops can be grown year round, that is enough. But in areas north of the Yangtze, where farmers can produce only one crop a year, the half-acre average is insufficient.

T RADITIONALLY, the peasant's response to the land shortage was to work hard, hoard his money and grain and, using this capital, try to rent or buy more land. The strong and shrewd who succeeded held on to their land and sought to expand it, so that they and their children might lead a more secure life, perhaps even the life of a landlord.

The Communists have put a stop to individual accumulation of land; they have, however, not been able to change the peasant's ingrained habit of thinking in terms of "my land". Nor have they been able to break his habit of trying to get the highest possible price for his produce, or of hoarding goods and money against the day when flood, famine or pestilence may bring disaster—or when land may again be bought and sold.

In view of this constant pressure for additional land, Communist concern about the peasants' "spontaneous tendency towards capitalism" is hardly surprising. An efficient grain-rationing system has prevented mass starvation in China. Yet forced redistribution of land, irrigation projects and elementary improvements in farming techniques have probably only barely succeeded in matching food production to population increase.

In recent years China's rulers have been forced to import large quantities of grain. Unless they can develop new techniques in crop production, birth control or land reclamation, China will find that its basic problem—too many people demanding too much from too little land—will remain unsolved for many years to come.

小甜水井街道居民劳动

A circus performer, balancing a pottery urn on his head, gives delight to an audience of children at a local exhibition of juggling.

Perplexing Figures Set in a Strange Landscape

China has puzzled Westerners since the Middle Ages. Over the centuries the Chinese, holding aloof from any culture rivalling their own, have preserved a unique way of life. Even now their language, costume and attitudes are at once distinct and elusive. Radical transformations brought about by missionaries and Marxists have failed to make China resemble the Occident. The same illusory element extends to the natural scenery. Factories may dot the countryside, but much of the landscape still appears to be rendered by a brush on faded silk.

17

HURRIED MERCHANTS of Shanghai pass a waiting line of
pedicabs—tricycle-mounted rickshaws. A port and commercial
centre Shanghai is the largest city on the continent of Asia.

DOTING PARENTS, members of a Uighur family, play with
their baby. The Uighurs, who are Moslems, are counted
among some 43 million non-Chinese peoples living in China.

WESTERNIZED CITY DWELLERS, preparing for a national holiday, plant flags in front of a modern apartment building representative of the living quarters going up in urban areas.

ATTENTIVE ATHLETES awaiting their event watch from the sidelines of a Peking stadium. China, striving to set records and improve health, follows an ambitious sports programme.

RESTING QUIETLY in the River Kwei valley below grotesque mountains, the small city of Kweilin lies in the southern rice-growing area that is marked by flat fields and twisted hills.

POLING HARDILY sailors navigate their junk into Chungking following a journey up the Yangtze. The shallows and rapids of the Yangtze make it the world's most treacherous river.

SWARMING THICKLY, boats, sampans, junks and rafts cluster along a Canton quay. Once citizens of such a "water city" never left their boats; now many work in town and country.

A MASSIVE DISPLAY of banners and slogans held by uniformed ranks of labourers and uniformed militiamen signals the last day of construction of the Ming Tombs dam in 1958. Thirty-five miles north-west of Peking, the reservoir and dam, named after the near-by tombs of the emperors of a Chinese dynasty, required the labour of countless workers. Not only peasants, but

also professors and top government and party officials, assisted in the menial tasks that were required in the gigantic construction project. Belonging to a larger power, conservation and irrigation scheme, this dam is one of 11 designed to check flood and drought, supply electricity, and water a million acres, much of which has been converted into agricultural land.

A MOUNTAIN SHRINE in North-West China includes 258 representations of Buddha overlooking the rolling countryside of western Kansu province. Known as Mai Chi Shan, or "mountain of the Hay Stack", the shrine was built starting around A.D. 500, was rediscovered in 1941 and has since been restored. The wooden passageways running along the cliff led monks to the different grottoes cut into the mountainside. Many passageways have decayed, but the sculptures and buildings that remain seem to evoke a feeling of eternity.

2

Dynasties of Legend and Power

ACCORDING to a legend that has been told in China for 1,600 years, the creator of the universe was a being called P'an Ku. Assisted by a dragon, a unicorn, a phoenix and a tortoise, P'an Ku laboured 18,000 years chiselling the earth into its present shape.

When P'an Ku died, his body underwent a marvellous transformation. His flesh became the world's soil, his blood its rivers, his sweat the rain, his hair trees and plants; his left eye turned into the sun, his right eye the moon; his breath became the wind and his voice made thunder. The legend also accounts for the parasites which were feeding on P'an Ku's body:

they became the members of the human race.

Despite this and many other theories, nobody knows where or when the Chinese originated. Certainly, men have lived in China for a very long time. The skull of *Sinanthropus pekinensis*, or Peking man, who lived in a cave on the North China Plain some 360,000 years ago, was found in 1929. Four years later, seven more cave dwellers were found near by. They belonged to a much more advanced species than Peking man and lived about 25,000 years ago. The links connecting Peking man and these later cave dwellers with each other and with the Chinese of historic times have not yet been found. Nevertheless these finds, and those of a series of archaeological excavations made since 1928, have demolished long-held theories that the Chinese were simply migratory offshoots of Middle Eastern civilizations.

The Chinese credit a vast array of legendary supermen with all manner of incredible accomplishments. Some of these heroes ruled over dynasties which endured for thousands of years; others supplied mankind with the essentials of civilized life. One Fu Hsi, whose dates some Chinese still seriously list as 4754 to 3495 B.C., was among the most versatile of the benevolent supermen. He taught man hunting, fishing, herding, writing, philosophy and music. Fu Hsi, or perhaps his mate, curbed promiscuous reproduction by instituting marriage.

Later came the legendary emperors—Yao, Shun and Yu—whose names Chinese immediately connect with flood prevention, powerful government and the creation of the Hsia Dynasty. But there is no historical evidence to prove that any of these rulers or their dynasties ever existed.

FOR many years Western historians tended to doubt whether Chinese civilization had existed for even 3,000 years, let alone the 5,000 most Chinese scholars claimed. Then the Chinese belief in the medicinal powers of "dragon bones" set off a series of events which put the doubters on the defensive. For centuries, Chinese herb doctors have ground up the bones or shells of animals and prescribed the "dragon bone" powder for the cure of a variety of ailments. Late in the 19th century, scholars in Peking noticed that some of the bones being supplied to herb doctors bore intriguing incised symbols. It soon became clear, to these savants' horror, that generations of ailing Chinese had been swallowing Chinese history in powdered form.

The symbols turned out to be Chinese characters used 3,000 or more years ago—the period when legends said that a dynasty called the Shang had ruled China; they had been carved into what proved to be tortoise shells and the

shoulder and leg bones of oxen. The inscriptions dealt with such questions as whether a harvest would be good or whether there would be victory in a forthcoming battle. The manner in which the bones split when heated provided the answers to the questions. The scholars traced these "oracle bones" to an area around Anyang, about 80 miles north of the Yellow River in Honan province. There lay a number of ancient graves. This seemed to be the basis for believing that a civilization had flourished in this area at least 1,000 years before Christ. But there was no real proof. The logical next step was scientific excavation.

FOR a time, however, it was impossible to take the logical step. Professional curio sellers and inscription forgers lobbied against excavations. Armed peasants in the area who made extra money scavenging graves threatened to kill government excavators. No authorized digging started until 1928. As late as 1934 a Cabinet minister, decrying the unfilial practice of opening graves, asked why these modern excavators should not face the ancient punishment for grave-robbers—death by slicing.

But the interests of science, and perhaps of modern nationalism too, prevailed. Working under cover of armed guards, excavators by 1937 had removed a fabulous treasure of archaeological and historical materials. From the loess soil of the North China Plain came indisputable evidence that the previously legendary Shang Dynasty had in fact existed—and that the people of Shang had achieved a high technological and cultural level.

Theirs was an agricultural society dominated by aristocrats. Animals were hunted and domesticated for skins and food. Skilled artisans erected elaborate buildings, some of them more than 90 feet long and nearly 30 feet wide, although some members of the society, perhaps slaves captured from neighbouring tribes, lived in earthen pits.

The people of Shang had the wheel and used chariots against their enemies. They wore silk and furs. One form of money or reward was cowrie shell brought from the East China Sea, 500 miles away. Art forms included bronze vessels, painted pottery and sophisticated carvings in wood, marble, limestone and jade.

Tens of thousands of "oracle bones" came from the Anyang diggings. They reveal a written vocabulary of some 2,500 individual characters and give China records going back more than 3,300 years. To be sure, neither the Anyang findings nor more recent excavations elsewhere have proved the existence of China's legendary heroes or of dynasties pre-dating the Shang. Legend says that a dynasty known as the Hsia reigned from about 2200 to 1700 B.C. as the immediate predecessor of the Shang. No material evidence of its existence has yet been identified. Yet the archaeological verification of the long-suspect legends of the Shang does suggest that the stories about the Hsia, and those about even earlier dynasties, might be just as valid as those of the later period.

In any event, China can be said to have the longest continuous history of any nation on earth. The valleys of the Tigris and Euphrates, the Indus and the Nile all produced civilizations before any that have been uncovered so far in China. But none of these other civilizations has endured. China, on the other hand, despite periods of war, chaos and foreign rule, has maintained a resilient cultural continuity.

In part because of this, history and tradition loom large in Chinese life. Leaders from the earliest times up to Chiang Kai-shek and Mao Tse-tung have acted on what they felt were valid historical precedents. In Chinese thinking, many of these precedents, found in official histories, date back to the Chou Dynasty, which succeeded the Shang in about 1100 B.C.

IN China, however, the official history of a dynasty was usually composed by authors employed by the succeeding dynasty. The desire to justify the overthrow of the earlier dynasty undoubtedly caused distortions in some of these histories. None the less a pattern became evident in the histories which was to be repeated so many times in later centuries that it

MAJOR DYNASTIES IN CHINESE HISTORY

SHANG (c. 1700-1100 B.C.): An agricultural society, it flourished in the Yellow River valley, had a highly developed writing system, and used wheeled chariots in warfare.

CHOU (c. 1100-256 B.C.): Its kings extended China's power to the Yangtze valley. Confucius and other sages flourished in the dynasty's declining years.

CH'IN (221-206 B.C.): A short-lived but dynamic dynasty, it rapidly succeeded in bringing all of eastern China under its domination.

HAN (202 B.C.-A.D. 220): Vigorous and expansionist, this dynasty vastly expanded China's borders and received tribute from kingdoms throughout Asia. So successful was the dynasty that to this day Chinese refer to themselves as "the sons of Han".

SUI (590-618): The Sui emperors recovered the territory lost after the fall of the Han and built a great transport network with millions of labourers.

T'ANG (618-906): In its early years, this dynasty expanded deep into Asia. Later less militaristic, it experienced a great cultural flowering.

SUNG (960-1279): Its emperors reunified the country after a period of disunity. Fine porcelains and landscape paintings were produced.

YUAN (1279-1368): The Mongols controlled China from Peking. The most famous of the Yuan emperors was Kublai Khan.

MING (1368-1644): Chinese culture flowered again under this native dynasty. Great fleets went abroad to obtain tribute and trade.

MANCHU (1694-1911): Invaders from the north, the Manchus brought China again under alien rule. For 150 years they expanded and strengthened the empire only to topple before foreign encroachment.

gave rise to a Chinese theory that history tended to follow ever-recurring cycles.

The cycle begins when the ruler of a dynasty falls into evil ways. Thus, according to an account circulated after his death, the last ruler of the Shang Dynasty originally had been a virtuous man, and so strong that he could kill tigers with his bare hands. Yet eventually he began to inflict "calamities on the people". In one version of the story composed in later centuries, Wu Wang, ruler of the neighbouring vassal state of Chou, asserted: "The King of

Shang does not reverence Heaven above and inflicts calamities on the people below. He has been abandoned to drunkenness and [has been] reckless in lust. . . . He has put men into office on a hereditary basis. He has constructed palaces, towers, pavilions, embankments and ponds, and engaged in many other extravagances. . . . He has burned and roasted the loyal and good. He has ripped open pregnant women."

To this recital of the tyrant's infamy, Wu Wang added: "He is contemptuous of the spirits of Heaven and Earth, and neglects the temple of his ancestors." The Shang monarch also failed to protect the gathering of the harvest. Therefore Wu Wang, who was to become the first ruler of the Chou Dynasty, declared: "The iniquity of the Shang is full. Heaven commands me to destroy it."

Wu Wang was supported by his officers and people. They overthrew the Shang, decapitated the king and executed the most hated of his concubines.

The story resembles the Shang legend of how its own founders managed to come to power by overthrowing a similarly debauched Hsia tyrant 600 or so years earlier. And here we see forming Chinese theories about change within tradition that have persisted into modern times.

THE pattern, as the Chinese saw it, was as follows: The ruler of a declining dynasty, frequently captivated by a depraved beauty, indulges in personal and state extravagances. He is cruel to his subjects, and relies on sycophants instead of virtuous advisers. He neglects the ancestral spirits and offends Heaven—which, in Chinese thought, was not God but an impersonal celestial presence. Corruption and rebellion are seen everywhere. From the chaos emerges a virtuous man who secures Heaven's mandate. A new, and for a time, vigorous dynasty is formed. But it too loses its dynamism eventually, and the cycle begins anew.

The early days of the Chou saw a rapid expansion of power, but after several centuries the state declined and its borders contracted. Confucius and the rest of China's most famous philosophers lived in this period of decline. The ideologies these men preached were conditioned by the disorder of their times. With the exception of the Taoists, who tended to seek refuge in nature or in supernatural pursuits (see Chapter 5), the philosophers were most interested in affairs of state. As the Chou dwindled among a cluster of warring states, these men sought practical solutions to the problems of government.

CONFUCIUS, who lived from 551 to 479 B.C., and Mencius, his disciple of about two centuries later, saw government as a problem in ethics. If a ruler conducted himself properly, his ministers would do likewise; if the ministers were upright, the people would be obedient and all would be right with the world. All men were basically good. The key to the good life was right conduct and observance of the proper relationships between superiors and inferiors. Inferiors were to give loyalty to superiors; superiors were to earn and retain loyalty by honest discharge of their duties and by benevolence towards inferiors.

Confucius and Mencius were much honoured, and their doctrines became widely influential, but not until long after both men had died. They spent their lives preaching their ethics to uninterested or powerless rulers. The philosophers who set the ideological stage for the great but short-lived dynasty that succeeded the Chou were a different breed—tough and cynical.

Hsun Tzu (*c*.300 to 237 B.C.) was a Confucianist with Machiavellian overtones. He believed that man was by nature inclined to evil. Only education—one that was based on a diligent study of classical literature—could overcome man's selfish and emotional inclinations. Hsun Tzu's disciples, Han Fei Tzu and Li Ssu, carried this disbelief in man's moral nature a step further.

Known as the Legalists, Han Fei Tzu and Li Ssu thought that whatever contributed to the state's power and might should be deemed

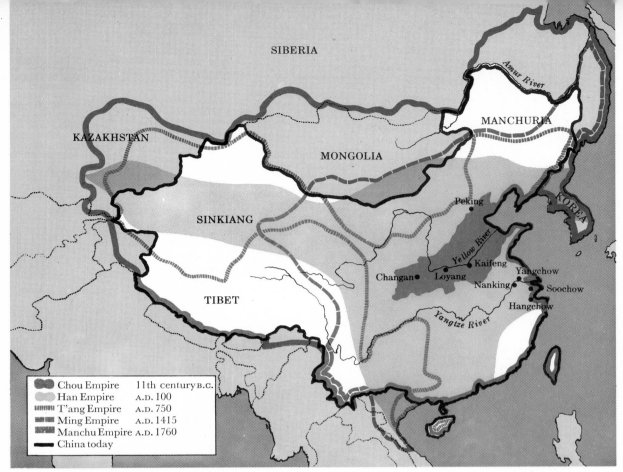

EXPANSION AND CONTRACTION in China over 3,000 years is indicated on the map above. From what is often considered the "heartland" held by the Chou Dynasty in the lower Yellow River area, the country expanded radically, reaching to the west under the Hans. It was at its largest under the Manchus in the 18th century before declining to its present borders.

right. Obedience to central authority, production from the peasants, efficient military and executive leadership—these were the principles underlying their philosophy.

Their thoughts found ready support in a western border state called Ch'in, a kingdom that had developed under the constant threat of raids by nomadic horsemen from what is now Inner Mongolia. In response, Ch'in early developed its own cavalry and an energetic centralized government modelled along military lines. By 256 B.C. its vigorous administrative and military system had enabled Ch'in to gobble up a number of minor states and finally to subjugate the declining Chou.

Li Ssu had migrated to Ch'in from the southeast in 247 B.C., and within 10 years he had become adviser to an ambitious and talented king. By 221 B.C. Ch'in's thundering legions had swept north and east to the Yalu and south to what is now Vietnam, gaining an

area which today would comprise China's eastern heartland.

The King of Ch'in presumptuously assumed the pretentious title *Shih Huang Ti*, or "First Emperor", and prepared to rule over what he boasted would be an everlasting empire. He extended the Ch'in system of centralized government throughout the new realm, dividing it into 36 military areas. In each area, triumvirates consisting of a military commander, a civil governor and a watchdog representative from the central government replaced the hereditary aristocracy. The displaced aristocrats became resident hostages in the Ch'in capital of Sienyang; cut off from their normal pursuits, they and their families formed the core of an important new "scholar gentry", dedicated to literature and the arts.

On Li Ssu's advice, Ch'in agents purged libraries of all but strictly utilitarian works. Books on history and philosophy were considered especially subversive. Scholars who protested were branded and sentenced to terms in forced-labour battalions.

Reforms accompanied the terror. Weights, measures and coinage were standardized. A uniform writing system, which has remained essentially unchanged to this day, came into use. Law and order prevailed. Peasants chafed under labour and grain levies, but within a few years Ch'in had united a mass of squabbling states into an empire commanding fear and respect. The goal of every subsequent government has been to erect a similarly feared, respected and united China.

ALTHOUGH Shih Huang Ti had established his empire by following the authoritarian Legalist doctrines of Han Fei Tzu and Li Ssu, to keep it everlasting he sought personal immortality by following magical Taoist practices. Regrettably, the charms failed, and China's first emperor died. Palace intrigue and regional revolt racked the empire. By 206 the Ch'in Dynasty had collapsed. It had lasted just 15 years.

The founder of the next dynasty, Liu Pang, was a petty village official of peasant stock who skilfully rode tides of peasant misery and aristocratic discontent to become a powerful guerrilla general. Smashing the last of his rivals in 202, he proclaimed himself emperor of the Han Dynasty.

In his years in power, Liu Pang made only one serious mistake: he restored some of the hereditary vassal kingdoms. In consequence, he and his heirs spent the next 50 years suppressing the vassals' defiance of central authority. Apart from this deviation, the Han rulers stuck close to the Ch'in system of government. Their methods, however, were somewhat milder. Labour and grain levies were reduced. The scholar gentry was increasingly well treated.

Later Han emperors established an imperial academy for the training of officials, set up a civil-service examination system and made Confucianism the official state doctrine. These three steps together helped to create a bureaucratic class which came to assume large importance in Chinese history. Since a knowledge of the Confucian classics with their emphasis on loyalty to superiors was essential to pass the exams, the bureaucracy became a reliable prop of the state and a force for conservatism and continuity. The absolutism and utilitarianism preached by the Legalists lingered on as the martial Han Dynasty expanded the state's frontiers, but Confucian ethics and benevolence made life bearable for its subjects.

The Han Dynasty was exploited by grasping empresses, treacherous eunuchs and scheming generals. Military campaigns striking as far west as the Pamir mountain range in Central Asia sapped the treasury. Increased levies, inflated currencies and famine brought on peasant revolts. Barbarians from the north at times surged through the Great Wall. But the system remained strong. The great Han Dynasty lasted (with one minor interruption) more than 400 years. Although the fact is seldom noted, the Han Empire was, in extent of territory, number of people ruled and level of culture, the equal of its contemporary to the west, the Roman Empire. When the Han, strained by rivalries among great landholding kingdoms at home and by barbarian attacks on the frontiers, finally disintegrated, almost four centuries of titanic military struggle and social unrest ensued. But at all times control of a unified China remained the paramount goal.

FORCES far more complex than those outlined in the oversimplified Chinese theory of dynastic cycles gradually pulled the empire together again towards the end of the sixth century. Absorption of hardy barbarian peoples with new ideas and ready minds reinvigorated Chinese society. The Chinese written language had remained standard throughout the area, facilitating administration. More important, the classics had continued to be the path to literacy and public office; these indoctrinated their readers with the concept of powerful, paternalistic central government.

In 581 a new empire began to emerge under the Sui Dynasty, and China began a period of political and cultural development spanning nearly 700 years and three great dynasties—the Sui itself, the T'ang and the Sung.

The Sui, like the Ch'in, attempted too much too quickly. Sui legions bled in expansionist campaigns in Korea, Central Asia and Vietnam. In little more than a generation the house of Sui burned itself out. But Li Yuan, a prominent Sui official of mixed Chinese-barbarian stock, stepped in quickly and established the T'ang Dynasty. China's influence soon extended as far as Mongolia, present-day Afghanistan and South-East Asia.

Cultural achievements at home paralleled military feats abroad. Blending Confucian tradition with influxes from India and Central Asian influences, T'ang became a golden age of poets, painters and learned men. A burgeoning economy supported skilled artisans, musicians and wealthy merchants. Even as T'ang military power began to wane in the eighth century, Chinese culture flowered, and it continued to flourish through the three centuries (960-1279) of the Sung Dynasty.

SOME Chinese have a tendency to be apologetic about the late T'ang and the Sung Dynasties, perhaps because fewer military successes were achieved during those periods than in the early years of the T'ang. China at the time was nevertheless the most advanced nation in the world. Contemporary Europe, embroiled in the Crusades, had few technological achievements that could compare with China's abacus, fine silks and lacquers, moveable type, paper money or explosives. Nor did Europe have anything remotely comparable to China's art and literature, or its highly cultured, homogeneous bureaucracy.

But the good life softened and divided Sung and attracted organized Mongolian hordes. Genghis Khan's cavalry cut out great chunks of northern China, turned west and took Central Asia. His descendants, employing Chinese collaborators, chased the last of the Sung emperors into the sea near Hong Kong in 1279. While Mongol bowmen terrorized Europe,

their cousins ruled China for almost a century.

The Mongols remained unassimilated, employing many Central Asian administrators. The Chinese bitterly hated the Mongols' crude ways and foreign domination. After Chu Yuanchang, a former Buddhist novice with a poor peasant background, organized a rebellion, expelled the Mongols from Peking in 1368, and founded the Ming Dynasty, Chinese culture rapidly asserted itself.

THE Ming Dynasty gave China great novels and exquisite porcelains. Huge Ming fleets prowled the South Seas and sailed as far as the East African coast. Perhaps in reaction to the domination of the alien Mongols, China in the same period developed a strong contempt for outsiders. The concept of China as the civilized centre of an inferior barbarian world grew and persisted into the 20th century.

Conquest by the Manchus, an alien people from what is now China's north-east, actually served to reinforce this view. After overthrowing the Ming Dynasty in 1644, the newcomers founded the Manchu, or Ch'ing, Dynasty. Yet unlike the similarly alien Mongols, the Manchus accepted Chinese culture. They ruled, but they ruled through Chinese officials and in the age-old Chinese way. Versed in the classics and official histories, all educated men looked backward on centuries of greatness. They saw no need for innovation.

To them, that view appeared sound. But there was a fatal oversight: the world outside had outstripped China technologically. "Barbarians" unlike any China had ever experienced came from the other side of the earth with weapons, opium, trade goods and ideas that nothing in the classics could cope with.

Traditional China collapsed at the end of the 19th century. Only now does a new empire seem to be emerging. It draws heavily on old ideas and institutions—the superiority of China and its ways to foreign customs and notions, unquestioned obedience to authority, a strong bureaucracy—but it is also experimenting with much that is new.

The Monumental Splendours of Peking

Peking has been the capital of China almost continuously since A.D. 1267. Over the centuries, as emperor after emperor added palaces and shrines, it became a glorious museum of Chinese art and architecture. The greatest concentration of these treasures lies within the oldest section of Peking, the Inner City. In the manner of Chinese boxes, the Inner City contains the Imperial City, which in turn surrounds the Forbidden City, the palace compound reserved for the court. Other parts of Peking also boast gardens and palaces, ranging from Jade Fountain Hill, an imperial hunting park in the 12th century, to the new Summer Palace, whose buildings date from the 19th. Everywhere there is evidence in stone, bronze and wood of the continuity of Chinese history.

A GRACEFUL PROMENADE known as the Painted Gallery curves for 1,170 feet along the lake shore of the Summer Palace, which lies seven miles north-west of Peking. The Summer Palace is an elaborate mixture of pavilions and parks, gardens and towers.

A BRONZE CRANE, which symbolizes both strength and longevity, stands before the Hall of Supreme Harmony, the largest of the ceremonial halls in the Forbidden City.

CAVORTING DRAGONS lash about in green waves on a Ming Dynasty bas-relief whose tiles retain their brilliant colours after more than three centuries. Called

AN ELABORATE MONUMENT, noted for its Hindu-style tower, is part of the famous Yellow Temple, a sanctuary near Peking which was for long a centre of Lama worship.

A STONE LION guards the Gate of Heavenly Peace, a principal entrance to the Forbidden City. According to legend, this lion warned emperors of official malpractice.

the *Chiu Lung Pi*, or the "Nine Dragon Screen", this 40-foot sculpture adorns a garden in the northern section of the Forbidden City known as the Winter Palace.

SLIM PAGODAS dominate the ruins of an elaborate pleasure garden built by Emperor K'ang Hsi between 1680 and 1692 on the site of an earlier hunting preserve.

THE INNER CITY
holds ornate temples
and scientific
equipment built
when Peking was
a centre of learning

AN ASTRONOMICAL DEVICE designed in the 17th century by the Jesuit astronomer Ferdinand Verbiest rests in a corner of "Watching the Luminaries Terrace", an observatory established by Kublai Khan.

A MAJESTIC DOME soars 50 feet over the Temple of Heaven. In it, prayers for a bountiful harvest were said. Such prayers were offered each spring on a date established by the imperial astronomers.

A CELESTIAL GLOBE, built for the Emperor K'ang Hsi in 1674, is still so perfectly balanced that its 2,000 pounds will revolve at a touch. The Chinese were accurate astronomers as early as the fifth century B.C.

A SAVAGE BREAK with China's age-old culture is reflected in Red Guards' defacing of great works of art

DISFIGURED BY TAR, a finely carved relief of Buddha seems to weep. Vandalism was by Red Guards, fanatical followers of Communist leader Mao Tse-tung. who would destroy China's past.

BANDAGED IN MATTING, a magnificent stone lion (see page 37) falls victim to the Red Guards, who believe that love of art and history weakens the zeal to create a revolutionary new world.

40

THE GREAT WALL of China, some 1,500 miles in length, once provided protection against invaders. It came into being in the third century B.C., when the Emperor Shih Huang Ti joined and extended walls previously built by feudal states.

3

Alien Contacts: Impact and Rejection

SINCE very ancient times the Chinese have considered their country the centre of the geographical and cultural world, a land surrounded by inferior barbarians. The very name by which the Chinese refer to their country reinforces this view. They call it 中國, which in English is transliterated as *Chung-kuo*. *Chung*, the first character, a rectangle evenly divided by a vertical line, means "central" or "middle"; the second, *kuo*, pictorially represents a wall around a camp and means "kingdom" or "country". So, from the time they learn to speak, the Chinese are inculcated with the idea that their land is the "Middle Kingdom", or the "Central Country"—the focal point of the universe.

The origin of the concept is rooted deep in Chinese history. More than 2,500 years ago, the prosperous agricultural communities of the Middle Kingdom became tempting targets for nomadic invaders from less prosperous areas. Many of these raiding tribesmen, especially those from the south and the east, were conquered or absorbed into the Middle Kingdom comparatively easily. More troublesome and far from absorbable were the tribes to the north and the west, particularly the fierce Hsiung-nu. They were the ancestors of the Huns who were to sweep deep into Europe in the fourth and fifth centuries A.D.

Living in an area of marginal rainfall and dreadful winters, the Hsiung-nu made frequent and savage raids on Chinese stockyards and granaries. Long before the King of Ch'in proclaimed himself China's "First Emperor" in 221 B.C., earlier rulers had erected isolated earthen walls to slow down or divert attacks from the Hsiung-nu and other barbarians. The Emperor repaired, garrisoned and connected these walls. Beyond the ramparts of his Great Wall, as it has been known to this day, he waged war on the barbarians. In the words of the great Chinese historian Ssu-ma Ch'ien, the Emperor managed to withstand the Hsiung-nu by "never keeping less than twenty or thirty thousand troops in the field, until the dead reached incalculable numbers, the corpses lay strewn for hundreds of miles, and streams of blood soaked the plains".

THE Hsiung-nu were formidable opponents. They "move on . . . swift war horses, and in their breasts beat the hearts of beasts", a general reported to a Han Dynasty emperor in 135 B.C. "They shift from place to place as fast as a flock of birds. Thus it is difficult to corner them and bring them under control." They had "never been regarded as part of humanity", the general went on, and he advised against continuing to struggle against them in the field. "It would not be expedient to attack the Hsiung-nu. Better to make peace with them."

The Chinese employed various methods for making peace. With barbarians too strong to crush, like the Hsiung-nu, they offered treaties sweetened by bribes of women and land. Often they attempted to manoeuvre the barbarians into fighting among themselves, and often with considerable success.

Sheltered behind their Great Wall, the Chinese developed a civilization unmatched by any of the peoples on their borders. Isolated throughout much of their history by distance, topography and the sea from peoples whose societies were comparable to their own, they came to feel more and more superior to outsiders as the centuries advanced. Eventually those feelings were to harden into a blinding self-admiration that prevented the Chinese from recognizing, centuries later, that the Middle Kingdom had fallen far behind at least some of the barbarians. Before that happened, however, the influence of Chinese culture and the news of China's wealth had spread far, attracting large numbers of travellers from the rest of Asia. An occasional visitor even reached China overland from Europe. Through the travellers China received much from the world outside the Middle Kingdom, and it gave much. Yet China failed to recognize the contribution of the outlanders; in Chinese eyes the visits simply reinforced the belief that the outside world had little to offer.

The first reports of other civilizations came to the Chinese as a result of the continuing struggle with the barbarian Hsiung-nu. About 140 B.C. the powerful Emperor of the Han Dynasty learned from Hsiung-nu captives that the Hsiung-nu had defeated a tribe to the west, the Yueh-chih and had turned the skull of the Yueh-chih King into a drinking mug. The remaining Yueh-chih had fled far to the west, looking for allies. The Han Emperor was eager to help the Yueh-chih to revenge themselves on the hated Hsiung-nu, and he therefore dispatched Chang Ch'ien, a trusted official, as an ambassador to the Yueh-chih.

CHANG CH'IEN'S journey was extraordinary. He travelled almost the breadth of Asia, enduring some 4,000 miles of sun-seared desert and blizzard-swept mountains. He was captured by the Hsiung-nu and fathered a son while their prisoner for 10 years. Eventually he escaped and found the Yueh-chih in what is now Afghanistan, only to discover that the old King's heir considered the Hsiung-nu "too far away to bother with".

Chang Ch'ien's mission was an ostensible failure. Nevertheless this explorer-diplomat returned with information of great value to the

Chinese. Most important were his accounts—some based only on hearsay—of places like India, the Persian Gulf, Parthia and Mesopotamia. The Han Emperor was impressed by these tales and followed them up with silk-laden missions to win the allegiance of countries reportedly "greedy for Han wealth and goods".

MANY diplomatic missions, often merchant groups only thinly disguised, reciprocated the Han overtures. But there were also rebuffs, and Han legions—defending the honour of the "Celestial Emperor" of the Middle Kingdom against the barbarians—eventually seized large areas in present-day Afghanistan and Soviet Uzbekistan. Contact between Chinese and Roman troops may have occurred in 36 B.C., when Han infantry on the River Talas north of Tashkent—a city now the capital of Uzbekistan—captured mercenaries whose shields, tightly overlapped in battle, suggested a "fish-scale formation". These were probably Roman legionnaires captured earlier by the Parthians, a powerful people who then held a large empire in south-west Asia.

Earlier exchanges between China and the Mediterranean area had been commercial and indirect. Silk, manufactured by the Chinese more than a thousand years before the birth of Christ, was the most exotic trade item, said to be worth its weight in gold. The Latin poet Horace, who fought at Philippi in Macedonia in 42 B.C., wrote of seeing silks and arrows there from Seres, the Roman name for the almost-mythical land of China. These had come from China via Central Asian middlemen. Describing the "baleful beauty" of Cleopatra a century later, the poet Lucan mentioned her "white breasts . . . revealed by the fabric . . . close-woven by the shuttle of the Seres".

At about the time Lucan wrote, one Chinese, sent to contact the Romans in Syria, got as far as Mesopotamia. The Parthians, fearing that a direct link between the Chinese and the Romans would cripple their profits on silk exchange, scared the envoy off with tales of dreadful travel difficulties. In A.D. 166 a number of "envoys"

claiming to have come from the Roman Emperor Marcus Aurelius Antoninus reached South China by sea, but very probably they were from the Middle East. There was never to be large-scale Chinese-Roman contact.

From the first to the eighth century A.D., however, a vast array of missions shuttled between China and other areas of the world. In 111 B.C., the Chinese had captured and annexed Vietnam. By the beginning of the third century, Chinese envoys had reached Japan, the South Seas, Ceylon, India and perhaps the Persian Gulf. Buddhism, one import destined to have a lasting effect upon China, was introduced into the Middle Kingdom during this period, almost certainly entering with missions bearing tribute from Central Asia.

Even in the chaos that followed the collapse of the powerful Han Dynasty in A.D. 220, the exchange of people and ideas did not end. Between 259 and 790, more than 180 Chinese monks made the long, dangerous pilgrimage to India, the home of the Buddha. In 641 a Chinese princess, a devout Buddhist, was married off to the king of Tibet; her influence helped to implant the religion there. In 648 Tibetan forces helped a Chinese mission to capture a troublesome Indian king. Between 713 and 751 ten Persian embassies visited China. In Changan, the capital of the T'ang Dynasty, they must have rubbed shoulders with Zoroastrians, Nestorian Christians, Manichaeans, Moslems and perhaps Jews. China in those early centuries was wide open to new religions and ideas of all kinds; among the new religions Islam was particularly strong.

A HISTORIC battle on the River Talas in 751 marked the finish of this great era of mutual exchange. There, Moslem troops defeated Chinese forces, and after that Chinese power in Central Asia waned.

But even in defeat ideas spread. Among the River Talas captives were Chinese skilled in making paper. The Arabs took these technicians to Samarkand, and from there the art of papermaking, which had been developed in

China a good 600 years earlier, spread to the Mediterranean and Europe.

In China itself the power and influence of Islam grew. In 756 Arab troops helped a young T'ang emperor to put down a serious rebellion, perhaps hoping thereby to keep trade routes open, and two years later Arabs took part in the sacking of Canton. By the end of the eighth century Arabs and Chinese were aligned against a common foe—aggressive Tibetans.

During the ninth century, the influence of new ideas waned in China. Chinese feelings of superiority to foreign barbarians reasserted themselves. Among the many foreign visitors to China at that time—Tibetans, Arabs, Vietnamese, Indians and Koreans—was Ennin, a Buddhist monk from Japan. Ennin kept a journal in China from 838 to 847. His and other contemporary accounts report the destruction of more than 46,000 monasteries and shrines and the enforced return to secular life of more than 400,000 Buddhist nuns and monks and their slaves. Similar repressive measures against some 3,000 Zoroastrians and Nestorian Christians were carried out. Foreign monks like Ennin were expelled, and on one occasion more than 300 Buddhists were executed.

Serious economic and administrative problems lay behind the persecution. Buddhist monasteries on great tax-free landholdings controlled hundreds of thousands of people who contributed nothing to government coffers. Criminals often bought sanctuary in monasteries. Exacerbating the secular problem was the long-smouldering hostility of the native Chinese faiths of Taoism and Confucianism. Their attacks contained anti-foreign appeals.

In 819 Han Yu, a Confucian purist, reported to the Emperor that Buddhism was "one of the practices of barbarians". He added: "Now Buddha was of barbaric origin. His language differed from Chinese speech; his clothes were of a different cut. . . ." Then, in prophetic outline of methods employed centuries later to handle outsiders, Han Yu hypothesized: "Let us suppose Buddha were living today, and that he came to court at the capital as an emissary of his country. Your Majesty would receive him courteously. But only one interview in the audience chamber, one banquet in his honour, one gift of clothing, and he would be escorted under guard to the border that he might not mislead the masses".

Buddhism survived the persecution. It maintained a firm hold on the masses and on later Chinese rulers as well. But the idea that foreigners were to be handled as potentially troublesome inferiors persisted well into the 20th century. There were, naturally, a few exceptions to the rule. During the Yuan Dynasty, when the alien Mongols ruled not only China but great chunks of Russia as well, foreign visitors were welcomed.

When the Mongol hordes first swept west into Europe in the 13th century, Christian leaders saw them as the "scourge of Heaven's wrath" erupting "from the secret confines of Hell". In time, however, that view changed. After all, reasoned some pragmatic Church politicians, the Christians who had fallen before the Mongols' arrows and blades were mostly undeserving Russians from the schismatic Orthodox Church. Moreover, some believed, the Mongols might possibly be converted and lined up to fight the infidel Moslems.

With alliance and conversion in view, at least three religious missions travelled to Mongolia between 1245 and 1260, but they had little success. The first real contact was established by

---

HOW CHINA ACQUIRED ITS NAME

Although the Chinese have always called their country *Chung-kuo*, "the Middle Kingdom", it has been known to the West by a variety of names. In the north, medieval Europe thought, lay a country known as "Cathay" or "Kitaia", after a people called the Khitan. In the south was "Sin" or "Chin", words derived from the name of the Ch'in Dynasty which united the Middle Kingdom in 221 B.C. In the 16th century Portuguese traders in South-East Asia began referring to the empire to the north as "China", and when Portuguese missionaries in Peking reported that "China" and "Cathay" were the same place, the term "Cathay" fell into disuse.

two famous Venetian merchants, the brothers Niccolò and Maffeo Polo. Travelling in what is now European Russia in search of business in 1262, they were prevented from returning to Venice by an outbreak of fighting among rival Mongol chieftains on their homeward route; they travelled east instead and reached the court of the mighty Kublai Khan in China four years later. The Khan received the two Venetians with great courtesy. The brothers so impressed the Khan that he entrusted them with a mission which, had it been successful, might have changed the whole history of Christianity.

KUBLAI KHAN offered a direct and challenging proposition: Let the Pope send 100 men learned in religion and the arts to his court. If these savants could prove the superiority of Christianity over other religions, then the Khan and all his subjects would be baptized. The Khan, with more accuracy than he perhaps realized, assured the Polos that there would then be more Christians in his realm than existed in all their part of the world.

When Niccolò and Maffeo got back to the Mediterranean in 1269 they learned that the Pope had died a year earlier. It took another two years to elect a successor, and the only wise men the new pontiff could provide the Polos were two Dominican friars. They had no inclination towards martyrdom and quickly abandoned the mission. So, when the two brothers returned to the Khan's court—accompanied this time by Niccolò's young son, Marco—they brought with them only some papal letters, gifts and holy oil from Jerusalem.

Marco was destined to eclipse his forebears completely. Kublai Khan, whom Marco later described as the world's "mightiest man, whether in respect of subjects or of territory, or of treasure", liked the bright young Venetian immediately. Marco served in the Great Khan's court for 17 years, travelling over much of China and into South-East Asia and noting carefully the marvels he encountered. Years later in Italy, Marco collaborated with a professional storyteller to put his notes and recollections together into a book grandiosely entitled *A Description of the World*.

While Marco was alive, few believed his tales and many ridiculed both the man and his book. But *A Description of the World* influenced the great voyages of discovery in the 15th century. Prince Peter of Portugal, elder brother of Prince Henry the Navigator, acquired a copy of it in about 1428; it was one of the inspirations for Prince Henry's captains in their search for a route to Asia around Africa. Columbus himself carried a copy of the book on his first voyage to America.

Although Marco Polo awakened great European interest in Asia and China, neither the Polos nor other Europeans of that period left much of an impression on China. Catholic priests made a few thousand converts, but after the Chinese drove out the alien Mongols and established the Ming Dynasty in 1368, virtually all traces of Catholicism disappeared.

Reacting to nearly a century of Mongol rule, the Ming rulers worked at restoring Chinese culture and traditions. But the early monarchs were by no means isolationists. Within 10 years of the founding of the dynasty, tribute embassies from Japan, Okinawa, Borneo, the Malay peninsula, Java, the Indian Coast and the Eastern Mediterranean were again paying their respects to—and trading at—Peking. Between 1405 and 1433 the Ming emperors sent seven maritime expeditions probing down into the South Seas and across the Indian Ocean.

THE Ming fleets, with as many as 62 huge ships and 28,000 men, were the most powerful task forces the world had ever seen. They made China feared and respected from Sumatra to the east coast of Africa. Their captains demonstrated a grasp of maritime organization and navigational skills not to be matched until nearly a century later, when the Portuguese fleets sailing around Africa reached China.

But after demonstrating this potential for ruling the seas, the Chinese abandoned the voyages. The expeditions had brought back interesting animals and even fearful kings bearing tribute from faraway places, but no Chinese seemed to realize their commercial and military value. Chinese officials, accustomed to relying on agricultural revenues, simply did not have the kind of aggressive economic and ideological outlook which was already stimulating European merchants, adventurers and missionaries to seek new empires.

The Chinese were not the only ones who failed to make the most of opportunities. Beginning in 1582, the Jesuits under Father Matteo Ricci made a concerted attempt to establish the Roman Catholic Church in China. But despite their persistence and brilliance, the Jesuits and the other Roman Catholic orders that supplemented them failed. A prime reason for their failure was the "rites controversy"; the Jesuits had attempted to work out a mutually acceptable blend of Christian theology and Confucian orthodoxy, but other missionary orders resisted the idea and in 1742 the Pope finally ruled against it. This strangled the Catholic missionary effort in China.

THE Catholics not only failed to convert China; they also failed to shake China's ruling class out of the inbred conviction that China remained the only civilized, powerful nation in the world and that barbarians were not worth bothering about. Yet at the same time, European knowledge of and interest in the Orient was developing. Eighteenth-century Europeans read Catholic translations of the Chinese classics. Rousseau and Voltaire debated accounts of Chinese history and government by students of China like Ricci. Rousseau did not like what he read, but Voltaire saw the morality and organization of the Chinese empire as "the best the world has ever seen". François Quesnay, a leading economic theorist of the day, wrote glowingly of benevolent Oriental despotism.

In a lighter vein, Europe went through a rococo artistic period strongly influenced by the Orient. Chinese latticework, pavilions, pagodas and gardens appeared everywhere. Many stately homes had special "Chinese" rooms where porcelains, lacquer-ware, wallpaper and furniture from China (and Japan) dazzled the eye. Thomas Chippendale even designed special "Chinese" rooms and furniture for his upper-class English clients.

More important, however, was European interest in trade with the East. The tales of China's great size and wealth stimulated the imagination and greed of empire builder and merchant alike. In 1793 the British, who had been trading regularly under aggravating restrictions at Canton since 1715, sent the astute Lord Macartney to Peking to persuade the Emperor to expand trade facilities. The experience of Macartney's mission demonstrates the isolation of China from the world of reality.

WHEN Macartney reached North China, the 83-year-old Emperor's councillors had already prepared a haughtily worded edict. It acknowledged King George III's "sincere humility and obedience" in sending a tribute mission to the Emperor. It also absolutely rejected the proposals for changing the existing trade arrangements since they did not "conform to the Celestial Empire's ceremonial system".

Macartney, together with visiting Mongols and Burmese, got one imperial audience and was given presents for his mission and the King. He received no state dinner and was escorted gently but firmly to Canton, where he sailed for London. The imperial edict he conveyed to George III declared China was self-sufficient and had "not the slightest need for your Country's manufactures". It also admonished King George to "act in conformity with our wishes by strengthening your loyalty and swearing perpetual obedience . . .".

At the end of the 18th century China was still conducting its exchanges with the West under the ancient concept of a superior central country dealing with inferior peripheral barbarians. It was a belief destined never to disappear completely from Chinese thinking—and one which is still perceptible in the attitudes and actions of the 20th-century leaders of the Middle Kingdom.

Sailing up the rapids, a long, low, flat-bottomed junk passes through the boiling, swirling eddies of the reaches of the Upper Yangtze.

Tranquil Points in the Cataract of Turbulence

The peasant has for long been an unwilling participant in politics—sons dragged off to war, grain collected for taxes, whole villages used for emergency labour. No matter how far from home he may wander, each Chinese dreams of that self-sufficient native village idealized by the ancient Lao Tzu: "Let the people regard death seriously and not move far from their homes. Though there might be boats and carriages, no one would go in them. . . . Let people be content with their food, their clothing, their houses, and with their customs." Such an independent spirit is maintained by those who live in tiny villages or work on the great Yangtze River.

HISTORIC CASTLES of the White Emperor's City dominate the Yangtze Gorges. Here in the third century A.D., according to legend, the heir to the throne protected himself from usurpers.

HARNESSED TRACKERS haul a group of boats through the Hsin rapids. The headman in black (*foreground*) instructs his workers while clowning with them to keep up their spirits.

A DRIFTING JUNK, safely out of the Yangtze Gorges, casts its reflection on the placid water. Feared for sudden floods, the Yangtze alternates between torrential and sluggish currents.

HEADMAN Chang and his wife, the leading couple of the Red Pepper Village in Hopei province, sit with dignified composure on a mat-covered platform, the *k'ang*. The platform, five feet wide and running the length of the wall, serves as bed, conversation corner and work area. A flue from the stove heats the *k'ang* in winter. The window panes are of translucent paper.

52

THE COURTYARD of the Chang household has the usual tool shed, pigsty and chicken house, as well as piles of corn, sorghum stalks and firewood. Beyond is the village's only street.

CITIZENS of the tiny community gather (*below*) in a village street. Twenty-eight families inhabit Red Pepper Village, typical of the communities where four fifths of the Chinese live.

MIXING PASTE of ground soya beans, the schoolteacher's wife prepares for winter. The North China diet, dull and lean, is interrupted only rarely by delicacies served at festival time.

FORMING DUMPLINGS, Mrs. Chang fills a large metal skillet. Housewives stretch as far as possible Red Pepper Village's scanty crops of corn, millet, wheat, sorghum and soya beans.

WINDING FIBRES, Mrs. Chang makes string by spinning a wood block that twists the plant filaments. Her feet are bound —evidence of a centuries-old practice that is now prohibited.

GRINDING CORN near the bamboo wall of his courtyard, the strongest man in town, "Rough" Ma, works with his daughter. Like his neighbours, Ma is a farmer, and he tills his fields which are part of the 50 acres cultivated by members of the community. Some villagers supplement their incomes by repairing roofs, making cloth shoes or selling pastries.

UIGHUR ACTORS in Sinkiang attend a rehearsal while a flautist practises (*background*). The Uighurs, agrarian people of North-West China, seek a greater measure of regional autonomy.

A GOLOK SCHOLAR reads a religious classic (*centre*) as a fellow herdsman stitches a jacket of yak fur (*right*). The Goloks, who live in China north-east of Tibet, revere the Dalai Lama.

A KIRGHIZ DANCER performs in Kashgar, a city not far from the Russian border in western China. Nomads of the Pamir steppes, the Kirghiz people are Moslems and speak a Turkic language.

in border areas, are fiercely proud of their languages, dress and sense of identity

涇陽不肯守孤城
單騎權為見雲行
扣馬力遠鄹睎誅生
芟手任葛羅擊吐

In a detail from a hand scroll attributed to Li Kung-lin, who died in 1106, a barbarian chieftain pays homage to a famous Chinese

The Flow of Brush and Pen

4

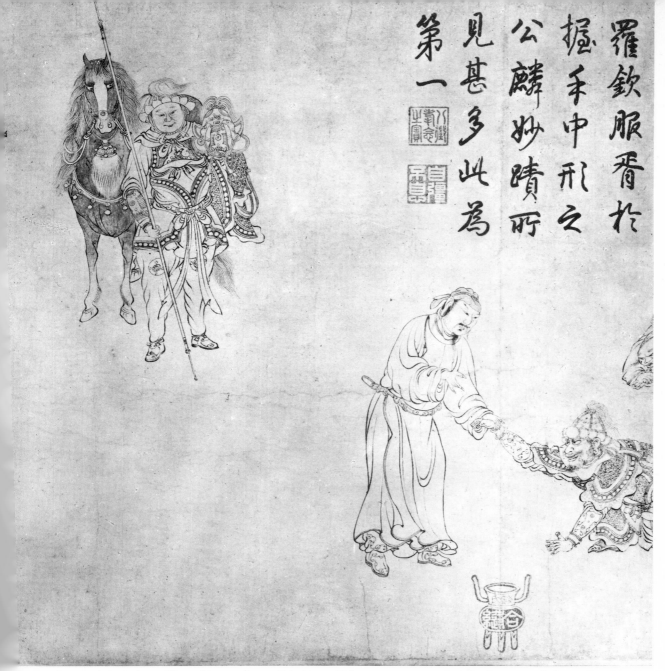

羅欽服香於
摳手中形之
公麟妙蹟所
見甚多此為
第一

general as retainers look on. The writing on the scroll is by an 18th-century emperor, who tells the story and also praises the artist.

TO sample the essence of the arts of China, take a fine landscape scroll to an expert calligrapher. Then watch as the master, with sure flowing strokes, brushes on an ancient poem. The practice has been followed for centuries in China itself, for there calligraphy, poetry and painting complement and enhance each other. Poetry and calligraphy have traditionally ranked as higher forms of artistic expression. Painting, in the Chinese view, is a natural extension of poetry and calligraphy. A man who is not proficient in writing characters with brush and ink cannot hope to compose poetry, nor can a man unfamiliar with poetry and calligraphy expect to move others by his painting.

For the uninitiated, Chinese and foreigner alike, the enjoyment of Chinese poetry presents very special difficulties. Language is an obvious barrier; it is a truism that poetry rarely remains poetic in translation. Moreover, without a vocabulary of at least 5,000 characters and a close acquaintance with history and literature going back some 2,500 years, not even a Chinese can appreciate all the nuances of classical poetry. Yet it remains true that some of its rhythm and lyricism can be savoured by the uninitiated Chinese and even, in translation, by a sympathetic foreigner.

Calligraphy, defined as freehand writing "in which the freedom is so nicely reconciled with order that the understanding eye is pleased to contemplate it", presents greater problems. Before the eye can acquire "understanding", it must first undergo a long period of training. This training used to begin in China when children started to write characters with a brush at about the age of six. Few foreigners, of course, ever received such training, and with the recent advent of mass education and the ball-point pen, the number of Chinese who are being properly trained to write with a brush is steadily decreasing. Consequently, calligraphy and poetry, by virtue of their very specialized characteristics, are today becoming esoteric arts reserved to an already small and shrinking minority.

THE appreciation of Chinese painting, however, is much less dependent on a grasp of language and history than is the appreciation of poetry and calligraphy. A person who may not be able to perceive what calligraphers call the "adventure in movement" characteristic of their art—because he has not spent thousands of hours copying the models of old masters—may still respond to the serenity inherent in a misty landscape painting.

Similarly, there is much that the non-specialist can enjoy in China's great treasury of other art forms—bronzes, ceramics, sculpture, architecture and literature. Sampling this treasury is relatively easy, for many fine pieces of Chinese art can be found in museums and private collections outside the country.

The sturdy bronze vessels and figures produced in the Chou and Shang Dynasties some 2,500 to 3,500 years ago probably hold a wider appeal than any other works of Chinese art.

For the scholar studying the dawn of Chinese civilization, they provide many clues to the nature of the societies which created them. Some of the bronzes bear dated inscriptions providing virtually indestructible records of military campaigns, hunting expeditions and weddings, and even of such mundane affairs as land sales. In addition to their historical value, the early bronzes also reveal a remarkably high degree of artistic development.

THE bronze vessels come in widely varying shapes. Many of them were apparently used in religious ceremonies and rituals. Some of the simplest are carefully scaled figures of elephants and rhinoceroses and were designed to hold liquids. Most intricate are vessels cast into the shapes of fierce, tiger-like beasts. Braced by their tails, they stand on their hind legs, their entire bodies ornamented with a virtual zoo of animal heads, reptiles and birds.

Late in China's Bronze Age, craftsmen started elaborating their work with handsome gold and silver inlay. These vessels and chariot fittings, together with earlier bronze pieces, have retained their remarkable beauty through the ages. In fact many collectors believe that their soft green and black patina—formed over the centuries by chemical reactions in the bronze—has made the Shang and Chou pieces even more beautiful today than when highly skilled artisans first cast them.

While the Chinese consider sculpture a lesser art than poetry and calligraphy, they are justly proud of the superb, stylized carvings which decorate the stone walls of family tombs built in Shantung province in the Han Dynasty some 2,000 years ago, and of the strange stone lions and fanciful monsters that stand guard over tombs built from the second to the sixth century in Shantung, Kiangsu and Szechwan. Impressive, too, are the great Buddhist grottoes hewn from solid rock in Honan and Shansi in the fifth and sixth centuries A.D., their walls lined with row upon row of mammoth Buddhist deities. In Buddhist temples, a few fine figures in lacquered wood stand out from a great mass of repetitious and baroque carvings.

China's most remarkable sculpture, however, came to light only three decades ago, when archaeologists at the Shang Dynasty excavation sites in Anyang unearthed a number of small marble and white limestone figures. Among the most striking of them are an owl-like bird with human ears, a squatting man and a reclining buffalo. Enormous skills were required to execute these figures, skills which clearly required centuries to perfect. Experts believe, therefore, that Chinese stone sculpture must date back more than 4,000 years.

The unique and stimulating art form that is Chinese landscape painting evolved at a considerably later time in history, during a long period of national strife. In the four centuries following the disintegration of the Han Empire in A.D. 220, China was racked by civil wars. In those troubled times, scholarly men who normally would have formed the *élite* of the civil service were frequently passed over in favour of men known for their military prowess. Sometimes the scholars did attain government posts, but since life at the court of a petty ruler of a warring kingdom was frequently both degrading and dangerous, these man of learning often shunned the official life for which their training had qualified them. Withdrawing to country retreats, they devoted their time and talents to painting, poetry, calligraphy, philosophy and the delights of wine and nature.

FEW of these intellectuals gave up public life altogether. Some returned of their own accord to serve men they considered just. Others were forced back into service, for in China then as now men who could read, write and reckon were in short supply. And when these men returned, they brought their paintings and their ideas with them.

In their rural hideouts the scholars had mulled over the problems besetting their age, often guiding or blending their thoughts with emerging Buddhist doctrine or older Taoist and Confucian teachings. Their poetry and their painting reflected their physical and mental environment—cloud-swathed hills looming high over a tiny, solitary fisherman; a village barely visible on the wooded banks of a turbulent stream—the peaceful union of insignificant man with mighty nature.

In time the works of these former recluses influenced the official world. Their once radical forms of art became more and more accepted as the norm. Landscape painting, often markedly impressionistic, became the ideal form of Chinese painting, and it has remained so through the centuries.

ONE of the most revealing testaments to the delights of painting was recorded in the fifth century by Tsung Ping, a Taoist: "And so I live in leisure and nourish my vital power. I drain clean the wine cup, play the lute, lay out the picture of scenery, face it in silence and, while seated, travel beyond the four borders of the land. . . . Sages and virtuous men of far antiquity come back to live in my imagination. . . . I gratify my spirit, and nothing more. And what is there that is more important than gratifying the spirit?"

For the painter and viewer alike, landscape paintings provided spiritual escape from the troubles of the mundane world. Tsung Ping was simply one of the first escapist artists to set down his principles in writing. Unfortunately, no paintings by Tsung Ping or other artists of this formative stage have survived, for the ravages of time and war have taken toll of their works, which were executed on delicate silk and paper. Even paintings from the T'ang Dynasty, a later (A.D. 618-906) and vastly more productive period, are rare. But art historians and copyists, often working centuries later, have preserved some of the legacy and legend of these men and their works.

Enshrined in T'ang history and later legend is Wu Tao-tzu, considered by many Chinese as the greatest painter the world has ever known. Born about A.D. 700, Wu Tao-tzu was a Buddhist artist who early on caught the eye of Ming Huang, the renowned T'ang Emperor. Ming Huang is perhaps better remembered for his debilitating infatuation with the charms of the luscious concubine Yang Kuei-fei, but he was also a devotee of poetry and painting. He installed Wu Tao-tzu as a court painter, and Wu obliged by executing hundreds of Buddhist murals, as well as paintings of generals, dragons and landscapes.

Wu's skill with the brush has become legendary. His treatment of wind and water is reported to have been so marvellous that when he painted waves they thundered all night along the shore. Some monks once treated him rudely, and so he painted a donkey on the wall of one of the monastery rooms. That night the monastery echoed with the sound of thudding hoofs, and the next morning the chastened monks found the room's furniture in splinters.

Today it is impossible to compare Wu Tao-tzu's paintings with the work of later artists. Everything he did is gone. Yet for centuries he influenced Chinese painting, and his rapid, many-faceted style became the standard by which later painters were judged.

ALMOST certainly, other Chinese painters whose works have survived were as good as or better than Wu Tao-tzu. But the judgment of history and legend is strong. Chinese art critics, like their colleagues in literature, have for centuries believed that antiquity and excellence are virtually synonymous.

The tenacity of this belief was indicated in 1961, when a collection of Chinese art treasures owned by the Nationalist government went on display throughout the United States. Of the exhibition's 112 paintings, not one was by an artist born after the founding of the Manchu Dynasty in 1644. More than half the paintings came from the Sung period (960-1279), or from even earlier dynasties.

Critics and their attachment to ancient works apart, Chinese painting had a universality which speaks to all with an eye for beauty. No list of suggested samplings could possibly satisfy any serious student of Chinese art, but experts would agree that even the briefest list should include such masterpieces as the spirited T'ang

horses of Han Kan, the haunting "ink-dot" landscapes executed during the Sung Dynasty by Mi Fei, and "Spring Festival on the River", a panorama of life in Sung times painted by Chang Tzu-tuan. The delicately detailed flowers and birds painted by Lu Chi almost five centuries ago in the Ming Dynasty would also be on such a list, as would the marvellously perceptive studies of insect and plant life executed by Ch'i Pai-shih, who died as recently as 1957.

While it is relatively easy to walk into a museum or leaf through a few books and obtain some idea of the glories of Chinese art, becoming acquainted with the wonders of Chinese literature is a bit more difficult. A century ago it was virtually impossible for all but a handful of Westerners to get more than a glimmering of what the Chinese had written. Now, thanks to the patient work of many scholar-translators, much of Chinese literature has become available to foreign readers.

All of the so-called Confucian classics have been translated. So have selections from many of the dynastic histories, which are generally far livelier than the Confucian canons. Chinese folk tales, romanticized histories and novels all make delightful reading in translation. Less delightful, but often starkly revealing and informative, is the protest literature which had its beginnings towards the end of the Manchu Dynasty in the early 20th century and which grew to tremendous, strident volume in the 1940s. Even some Chinese poetry, rendered into Western languages by sensitive and gifted scholars, retains much of the feeling and colour of the original.

FOR more than 2,000 years, an extremely conservative concept of what constitutes literature dominated the Chinese literary world. The primary criterion was the Confucian tenet that a piece of writing should exert a beneficial influence on society and the state. China's pioneer historian, Ssu-ma Ch'ien (*c*.145-90 B.C.), bowed to this concept when he dutifully, and probably inaccurately, reported that Confucius

FURNITURE OF GRACE AND DIGNITY

Chinese court furniture is well known for its elaborate ornamentation, but the furniture used in Chinese homes is characterized by simplicity, dignity and sobriety. Unlike many Asian peoples, the Chinese use chairs as well as low stools and cushions, and the chair shown on the left is typical in the grace and delicacy of its design. Many Chinese chairs, like this one, are built high so that the feet rest not on the floor but on the lower rung. Household altar tables, such as that on the right, also have plain yet elegant lines—and just enough ornamentation to set them apart as religious objects.

had gone through some 3,000 poems, making a selection of those which "would be serviceable for the inculcation of . . . righteousness".

Originally folk songs, religious odes and dynastic chants, the 305 poems supposedly chosen by Confucius are included in the *Shih Ching*, or *Book of Poetry*, one of the Confucian classics. They are considered literature of the highest order, and many are delightful. But to justify their inclusion in the classics, scholars produced "commentaries" which often seem far-fetched.

Here, for example, is a short poem from the *Shih Ching*:

The sun is in the east.
That beauty is a lady.
She is in my house,
In my house.
She approaches me ritually, and I accept her.

The moon is in the east.
That beauty is a lady.
She is in my bedroom,
In my bedroom.
She approaches me ritually, and I make
  off with her.

Despite the ambiguity in the original Chinese and in any translation, it is difficult to believe that this poem originally expressed much more than reminiscence of a passionate tryst. The commentary in the *Book of Poetry*, however, says that the poem "attacks decay. . . . The

relation of ruler and minister was neglected. Men and women, mixing immorally, were unresponsive to the rules of propriety."

One section of the British scholar Arthur Waley's fascinating book *The Life and Times of Po Chu-i* illustrates the seriousness with which the Chinese took their literature. Writing to a friend on the principles of poetry, Po Chu-i, a renowned T'ang Dynasty writer, described his struggles for education and with the didactic use of literature. At the age of four or five, Po Chu-i relates, he learned to compose poems. He first heard of the civil-service examinations some 10 years later and crammed from then until he was 26. Employing some poetic licence, he writes: "I allotted no time for sleep or rest, with the result that I developed sores in my mouth and . . . my hands and wrists swelled."

Po worked his way up the official ladder, and by "reading histories and other books I always tried to discover the principles underlying good government. It was then that I reached this conclusion: the duty of literature is to be of service to the writer's generation; that of poetry to influence public affairs."

The examination system forced a narrow, intensive style of scholarship upon students and writers, but fortunately it did not stultify the growth of literature. The system ignored writing which failed to instruct ruled and rulers on their proper roles, although scholars frequently strayed from the orthodox path. Many an official anonymously put into book form colourful tales supposedly based on history. Chinese storytellers to this day have fascinated largely illiterate audiences with such stories. The action and intrigue of *Romance of the Three Kingdoms*, the most famous of these pieces of historical fiction, have made it a boyhood favourite of untold millions, including a Hunanese peasant lad named Mao Tse-tung. The book dramatizes the plotting and fighting in China as the Han Dynasty disintegrated. Another famous tale is the novel which has been translated by the Nobel Prizewinner Pearl Buck into English under the title *All Men Are Brothers*. It tells of bandits who heroically rebelled against corrupt government in the 12th century.

LIKE Renaissance Europe, the T'ang Dynasty required that the well-rounded man be as much a master of the poetic arts as of practical politics. Unlike the Europe of the Renaissance, however, China laid great stress on conformity and conservatism. Nevertheless creativity frequently overcame conformity in the scholar-politician. When this happened, poetry of deep feeling and beauty came into being. The poetic flowering of the T'ang has been most effectively preserved in a slim volume entitled *Three Hundred T'ang Poems*. Selections from this poetry primer have become so widely known that even illiterate country women lull babies to sleep with lines of T'ang poetry.

More than one young Chinese has thus obtained an introduction to the glories of Chinese poetry from this collection, for it contains excerpts from the works of both Li Po and Tu Fu —China's greatest poets.

Born in A.D. 701, Li Po had won a reputation as a gifted poet by the age of 15. Later in life he also acquired considerable renown as a hot-tempered duellist and a man exceedingly fond of the ladies. Li Po wrote and drank his way in and out of the court where the talented emperor Ming Huang and his pleasure-loving concubine Yang Kuei-fei encouraged art in all its forms. Yet for all his bravado and drunkenness, the poet is probably best remembered for tender poems like his "Night Thoughts":

> *Bright shines the moonlight at*
> *the foot of my bed,*
> *Perhaps reflected from frost on*
> *the ground.*
> *Lifting my head I gaze at the bright*
> *moon,*
> *Bowing my head I think of my family*
> *home.*

Tu Fu, a younger contemporary of Li Po, also showed early literary promise. He nevertheless failed his first imperial examination and never received a post he considered worthy of his talents. Proud, high-principled and outspoken, Tu Fu became increasingly bitter as he grew older. He often decried the harsh demands of war and attacked extravagances. Above all Tu Fu protested against the decadence brought about by corrupt ministers and the rapacious relatives of the royal concubine. One of his most famous poems first describes the orgiastic feasting in the court and then contrasts it with life outside:

> *Behind the red lacquered gates,*
> *wine is left to sour, meat to rot.*
> *Outside these gates lie the bones of*
> *the frozen and the starved.*
> *The flourishing and the withered are*
> *just a foot apart—*
> *It rends my heart to ponder on it.*

While poetry has always been the most honoured form of literature in China, writers have also produced notable works in other fields. The roots of drama go back to the rituals and music of pre-Confucian times, but the "Chinese opera" dramatic form dates from the Yuan Dynasty (1279-1368). Presented on a bare stage by actors in elaborate costumes, Chinese opera tells folk tales and familiar stories by combining highly stylized gestures, dance movements and dialogue with songs and musical accompaniment. Fiction dealing with the exploits of supernatural beings appeared in the T'ang Dynasty. In the Ming Dynasty, Wu Ch'eng-en produced an intriguing allegorical work whose hero is a stone monkey. A satire on the bureaucracy of Wu's time, the overt theme revolves around the adventures of this monkey who helps a Buddhist priest to overcome supernatural obstacles on a pilgrimage to India.

The first realistic novel of Chinese life, an anonymous work entitled *Chin P'ing Mei*, appeared in the 16th century. In some places so pornographic that one 20th-century English translation has many passages in Latin, this lusty, immensely popular book is a compelling exposure of human greed and frailty. *Dream of the Red Chamber*, a novel by two 18th-century writers, is more refined, though best known for its lachrymose presentation of love and tragedy.

While the majority of scholars served as officials under the Manchu conquerors after their arrival in the 17th century, anti-Manchu feeling still ran deep. Personal frustration was manifested in a number of novels like Wu Ching-tzu's *Unofficial History of Officialdom*, which satirized the corruption of the Manchus. The overthrow of the Manchus in 1911 set the stage for a flowering of Chinese literature.

The new movement resulted in part from the efforts of two young scholars, Hu Shih and Ch'en Tu-hsiu, to write Chinese in the vernacular. Until the 20th century most Chinese writing was composed in a formal literary language that was much more concise than spoken Chinese. Read aloud to a listener unfamiliar with the text, a passage in literary Chinese was virtually unintelligible. In 1917 Hu Shih and Ch'en Tu-hsiu correctly saw that a vernacular literature could quickly spread knowledge and break the conservative influence of tradition.

THE *pai-hua*, or vernacular writing, movement which they launched touched off three decades of great literary activity. Borrowing heavily from Western and Russian models, the polemicists of China's literary revolution wrote to undermine the old society. Satire was the main weapon. In *The True Story of Ah Q*, Lu Hsun—who was perhaps modern China's greatest writer until his death in 1936—tells the story of a simple-minded peasant who ultimately comes to symbolize China itself. Ah Q, the peasant, acts superior towards his tormentors, rationalizes victory out of defeat and finally is wrongfully shot as a thief.

SINCE the Communist takeover, the literature of protest has been ground out of existence. Some two decades ago, Mao Tse-tung led a series of discussions which have been published under the title of *Talks at the Yenan Forum on Art and Literature*. The talks were long, but the message was simple. "If you are a proletarian artist or writer," Mao said, "you will extol not the bourgeoisie but the proletariat and the working people."

In the spring of 1957, with the words "Let a hundred flowers bloom, let a hundred schools contend", Mao himself invited China's writers to criticize the work of government and party officials. When that criticism got too pointed, the Communists cracked down, labelling critics "rightists" and "counter-revolutionaries". In Communist China today, therefore, the once outspoken critics again do what they must: they keep silent or they woodenly extol the party. Artists specialize in bountiful commune scenes or do portraits of Chairman Mao receiving the adoration of the masses.

On Taiwan, artists and writers are less restricted and a few show promise, but out of long experience they are cautious. They know that zealous Nationalist censors have difficulty in distinguishing between legitimate criticism and covert Communism. In Hong Kong, and in other overseas Chinese congregations, there is little notable artistic development. The creative forces unleashed by Hu Shih and Ch'en Tu-hsiu in 1917 have everywhere atrophied since Communist orthodoxy triumphed on the mainland in 1949. A great Chinese cultural revival seems unlikely soon. But when such a revival does come, the writers and artists of that time will have a magnificent heritage to draw on to depict the tragedy and pathos of China in the first half of the 20th century.

A gracefully modelled swallow, its wings spread in flight, surmounts a bronze ceremonial wine vessel cast during the Shang Dynasty.

Three Thousand Years of Splendour in Art

The earliest great era of Chinese art known today came at the dawn of history, during the second millennium before Christ, and produced the splendid Shang bronzes. A second flowering of the nation's art began hundreds of years later with Chinese painting. By the 12th century A.D.—before Europe's own Renaissance—China had many painters unsurpassed for their mastery of line, colour and proportion. Their ideal was to render the controlling idea of Chinese philosophy and religion—the basic harmony of nature and man. This idea of harmony also led the Chinese to create other masterpieces—graceful pottery and porcelains which took their forms from plants and animals and brought an ideal of beauty into everyday life.

A FANGED TIGER, executed in bronze by an unknown artist of the Chou Dynasty in the 10th century B.C., seems to epitomize animal ferocity. Now in the Freer Gallery in Washington, D.C., this 10-inch-high figure is a rare example of the small but powerful animal sculptures which were characteristic of a particularly vigorous period of China's Bronze Age culture.

BIBULOUS LADIES become tipsy (*above*) to the music of flute, lute and zither in a silk scroll which dates from the 10th century A.D.

A JAGGED LANDSCAPE, bold but unrealistic (*opposite*), is believed to be an 11th-century copy of a design dating from the T'ang Dynasty.

HARDY FISHERMEN pole boats in a detail from a 10th-century scroll attributed to Chao Kan, who was justly famous for his river scenes.

A MAGNIFICENT SCROLL of eight horsemen riding in a park is believed to be the work of Chao Yen, son-in-law of a 10th-century Emperor of the Five Dynasties period. Executed on silk in ink and water-colour, this work demonstrates—in the spacing of the riders, the tree and the balustrade—the mastery of proportion common to the best of early Chinese painting. Many such scenes were painted by government officials accomplished in the arts as well as in administration.

*FINE STUDIES of
landscapes and
of animals and flowers
mark the work done
by two great masters*

A SWEEPING VISTA, dotted here and
there with infinitesimal figures (*left*),
is characteristic of the work of the
10th-century painter Tung Yuan, one
of a group of painters who emphasiz-
ed nature rather than human figures.

A DETAILED SCENE of wild birds,
grass and flowers shows the gentle
touch of Lu Chi, a 15th-century
Ming Dynasty court painter. Many
Chinese paintings carry inscriptions
and the red seals of their past owners.

TRANSLUCENT WARE, dating from the 15th century A.D., is made of clay so thin that the Chinese refer to it as "bodiless". The strong shadow of the brush can be seen through the sides of the bowl.

CRACKLED GLAZE characterizes the porcelain of two masterpieces (*opposite*) of the Sung Dynasty. The crackling in both the lotus bowl and gourd vase were not accidents but carefully achieved effects.

A SMALL STEM-CUP, decorated with a gracefully rendered peach, is from the Ming Dynasty (1368 to 1644) like the bowl above. Whereas earlier ceramists allowed flaws, Ming taste demanded perfection.

Buddhist priests perform a devotional ceremony in a Peking temple. Mahayana Buddhism, one of China's three principal religions, was

introduced into China from India during the first century A.D.

5

Mingled Faiths and Philosophies

IN his early youth Mao Tse-tung, the high priest of Chinese Communism, was a devout Buddhist, and he also used to quote the Confucian classics in arguments with his domineering father. Even after he had abandoned Buddhism and had begun to toy with Marxism at Peking University, Mao occasionally visited the neighbouring province of Shantung to view Confucius' grave and the birthplace of Mencius, Confucius' disciple.

Raised by a devout Buddhist mother, Chiang Kai-shek, leader of the Chinese Nationalists, has also been for many years a student of the Chinese classics. Converted to Methodism after his second marriage in 1927, and now a constant reader of the Bible, Chiang nevertheless built a Buddhist temple in his native village in 1931 in honour of his mother. One of Chiang's favourite philosophers is Wang Yang-ming, a Ming Dynasty neo-Confucianist who was influenced by Buddhism. A native of Chiang's own province, Chekiang, Wang Yang-ming stressed meditation

77

and intuitive knowledge as a guide to action. When faced with a crisis, Chiang often retires to the mountains or to the seaside to meditate before deciding on a course of action.

Mao and Chiang have not been the only Chinese attracted to two or more of the various beliefs that have flourished in China. Indeed, holding an interest in the classics and in widely divergent faiths is an ancient and honourable tradition in China. One example from the past is that of Chang Jung, who lived from A.D. 443 to 497. Chang began his official life as a secretary to a prince. Later he was captured by bandits while *en route* to a government post in distant Vietnam. As the bandits prepared to behead him, Chang sat quietly writing poetry. Impressed by his calmness, the bandits released him. Chang spent his later years as a renowned poet and royal confidant, a man who had made his mark in the world. But he had also acquired an abiding concern about the other world. As he lay dying, he asked that the Confucian *Classic of Filial Piety* and the Taoist *Classic of the Way and the Power* be put in his left hand. For his right hand he requested a collection of Buddhist scriptures.

SO common is this often overlapping multiplicity of faiths that the Chinese have a standard explanation of the phenomenon for curious foreigners: When a man is in a position of authority he is a Confucianist, because that doctrine supports the *status quo*. Out of power or office, a man becomes a Taoist, because Taoism deprecates both worldly authority and individual responsibility. As death approaches, a man turns to Buddhism, because that faith offers hope of salvation.

Over-simplified as it is, this explanation none the less helps to illustrate the fact that for thousands of years combinations of beliefs have been the rule rather than the exception in China. Not only have individuals taken what they wanted from several faiths when they wanted it; often the faiths themselves have borrowed beliefs and doctrines from each other. Almost every major town in China used to have a temple dedicated to a god known as Ch'eng Huang, patron of cities. Ch'eng Huang is customarily identified as a Taoist deity, but his name crops up in records dating back to the Chou Dynasty, which flourished long before anything called Taoism appeared.

IN some Taoist temples, the walls are decorated with frescoes depicting Buddhism's Ten Courts of Hell and other scenes associated with Buddhist doctrine. On Taiwan the priests of some Taoist sects say they are followers of Buddha, since the term for Buddha has come to mean any spiritual force.

Buddhism, Taoism and Confucianism have all shared one ancient and deep-rooted practice: ancestor worship. While it is common to associate Confucius with ancestor worship, Chinese were praying to their forebears hundreds of years before Confucius was born. From the Shang Dynasty oracle bones, historians are certain that men living along the Yellow River 3,500 or more years ago made elaborate sacrifices to their ancestors.

From Shang times to the 20th century, ancestors have been considered active, effective spirits. Generations of Chinese have believed that their forebears could influence every aspect of their daily lives from farming to warring, from marrying to child bearing. Prayers and sacrifices to ancestors have been a natural form of worshipful insurance.

Although the teachings of Confucius did have a major influence on the practice of ancestor worship, the Master himself was primarily concerned with other matters. Born, tradition says, in 551 B.C. in what is now the province of Shantung, Confucius lived during a period of almost constant warfare between petty kingdoms. A scholarly man appalled by royal venality and corruption, he sought to establish an ethical system by which the state could be properly governed and under whose precepts men could live in probity and honour.

In the ideal Confucian system, the relations between the rulers and the ruled were to be patterned on the relations between the senior and junior members of a strongly patriarchal family. If parents and elders, by adhering to a prescribed ritual and code of conduct, set the proper example for children to follow, then the children would respect and obey them. The family would be harmonious and its members would prosper. Similarly, if rulers were irreproachable in their personal and public conduct, they would gain the loyalty and obedience of their subjects, and the state would likewise prosper.

Confucius drew his philosophy from what he believed were the best traditions of the ancient Chou Dynasty. These traditions had included the ritualistic veneration of ancestors living or dead. Although Confucius apparently doubted the efficacy of worshipping departed spirits—"Unable to serve living men," he once asked, "how can you serve spirits?"—he strongly believed in veneration of authority. He therefore encouraged the practice of all ritual which encouraged conformity to authority.

Confucius did not live to see his philosophy put into practice. But later disciples obtained positions of influence at the courts of emperors who found Confucian doctrine useful in consolidating their rule. Eventually Confucianism put down deep roots in Chinese society. For more than 2,000 years the ideas of Confucius, reinforced by ancestor worship and the concept that the emperor was the "Son of Heaven" mediating between the spirits above and the people below, secured remarkably long periods of stable government for China.

CONFUCIANISM underwent many changes in the course of history. Many of these changes would never have met the approval of the Master himself. Like other visionaries of other times and other countries, Confucius would have been outraged by the excesses later committed in his name. He himself came to be regarded by some as a deity, or at the very least as a spirit worthy of veneration. Confucianism, the philosophy of stable government by virtuous superiors for the benefit of obedient inferiors, at times became a rationalization for tyranny. In the name of Confucian stability and their divine rights as representatives of "Heaven", despotic rulers many times crushed anyone who dared to question authority.

Such corruptions of Confucianism did not, however, go unopposed for long. The moderation and ethical concepts which Confucianism inculcated were powerful forces. Since virtually every educated person in China was schooled in the Confucian classics, the Master's exhortations to virtue exercised a restraining influence even on would-be evil-doers. Those same moral concepts encouraged principled men to oppose violations of the Confucian ethic. Moreover, the proponents of the ethic held dominant posts through the years. History, like popular journalism, has made the sometimes bloody transgressions of evil rulers far better known than the long, quiet periods when Confucian moderation kept both ruler and ruled in line.

CONFUCIUS was by no means the only sage to exercise a lasting influence on China. One night in 666 B.C., so one legend goes, a woman in the kingdom of Ch'u cried out in admiration at the sight of a falling star and immediately became pregnant. Sixty-two years later she gave birth to a white-haired child fully capable of speech. Later known as Lao Tzu, meaning the Old One or Old Sir, this sage eventually became disgusted with the sordidness of the Middle Kingdom. At the age of 160, he boarded a cart drawn by a black ox and headed westwards.

The guardian of a strategic pass along the Yellow River, sensing that a wise man was about to leave the world, asked the traveller to stop and record his thoughts. Thereupon Lao Tzu wrote out a volume of 5,000 characters. The primary Taoist work, the *Tao Te Ching*, known in English as the *Classic of the Way and the Power*, is said to embody the essence of those 5,000 characters.

Like most legends, this one has a number of variations, and all of them are wide open to question. But legends and works of disputed authorship can have as much effect on people and history as do hard facts and unquestionable documents. And since there is no conclusive evidence that Lao Tzu did not exist, it seems not only convenient but reasonable to accept Lao Tzu both as a man and as the author of the *Tao Te Ching*.

Despite the legendary antiquity of its basic book, Taoism did not burst forth upon China as a fully developed philosophy. Its origins are fantastically complex, as is Taoism itself. In *The Parting of the Way* the American scholar Holmes Welch puts the matter succinctly: "There is, in fact, no book to which the public can turn for a satisfactory summary of the Taoist movement in all its major aspects."

The simple term "Taoism", for example, means all sorts of things. Many people would say that it means the philosophy or religion of *Tao*, the "Way" of nature. That is a fair approach, but already one problem appears. Is Taoism a religion, or is it a philosophy? The answer is that it is both—and more than both.

Taoism existed as a philosophy long before Taoism the religion came into existence, and it continued to thrive as a separate philosophy later. But many other things are also part of Taoism—among them alchemy, trances induced through breath control, sex orgies and revolutionary religious movements. Clearly, these elements have little or nothing in common with each other.

Some roots of Taoism stretch back to China's prehistory and are faintly discernible in the beliefs and practices of medicine men. The philosophical tenet that men should seek to place themselves in tune with the endless rhythm of nature and forgo pointless striving

A RELIGION'S SYMBOLIC EMBLEM

Taoism, the religion-philosophy which traces its roots farther into antiquity than any other Chinese belief, has for long utilized this

gracefully bisected circle as its basic symbol. Taoism postulates that there are two primary forces constantly at interplay in the cosmos; one is the passive, female principle, Yin (*black*), and the other the active, male principle, Yang. There is no conflict between these complementary forces. Man and the universe are in harmony when both follow the *Tao*, or "Way", of nature, as dark complements light, and evil, good.

probably dates from the later centuries of the Chou Dynasty. By then disorganized tyrannies had displaced well-ordered government. While Confucius idealistically advocated a return to the well-regulated system of the early Chou Dynasty, Lao Tzu and later philosophical Taoists wanted as little as possible to do with formal rule. As the Harvard University scholars Edwin O. Reischauer and John K. Fairbank point out in their book *East Asia: The Great Tradition*, "The political ideal of the Taoists was a small state from which the cocks and dogs of a near-by state could be heard, but whose people were so contented that none had ever bothered to visit this neighbouring village. Their recipe for rule was to empty the people's minds and fill their bellies."

These naturalistic political ideals and the more introspective aspects of philosophical Taoism had wide appeal. They won interest not only from peasants who wanted to be left alone to till their fields; they also attracted intellectuals weary of Confucian restraints on the individual. It is not surprising that many men who as officials were good Confucianists escaped into Taoism on retirement.

In Chinese folklore and history Taoists are commonly associated with the search for elixirs of immortality. This was a late development in Taoism, for neither Lao Tzu nor his most respected disciple, Chuang Tzu, encouraged striving for immortality. Both seemed to look favourably on a natural long life, but neither sought to evade death. Chuang Tzu saw life and death as part of nature's way, affording "occasions for joys incalculable. . . . Early death or old age, beginning or end, all are good."

Not all Taoists were equally high-minded. Among the earliest and most famous of China's charlatans were two Taoist magicians, Hsu Fu and Lu Sheng. It was they who infected the ruthless but gullible Shih Huang Ti, China's "First Emperor", with the idea that he could become immortal. One of the Emperor's last acts was to kill a large fish that was said to be barring the way to the fancied P'eng-lai islands, where a death-preventing drug was reputedly to be found.

ANOTHER remarkable Taoist, Li Shao-chun, turned up at court a few generations later, and in 133 B.C. the Emperor Wu Ti commissioned him to turn cinnabar, the major ore from which mercury is produced, into gold. The idea was that by eating from dishes made of the newly created gold the Emperor could gain longevity and gradually proceed from there to immortality. Although Li failed to produce either gold or immortality for his Emperor, he was the first in a long line of alchemists whose experiments contributed greatly to Chinese pharmacopoeia.

Another first—the earliest mention of a Taoist god—is also connected with Li Shao-chun. Whenever Li began an attempt to transmute cinnabar into gold by heating it, he offered sacrifices to a divinity named Tsao Chun or Tsao Wang, Lord or King of the Stove. Tsao Chun is still one of the most popular of the dozens of Taoist deities in China. His picture is hung in millions of homes. As the Hearth God, Tsao Chun watches the household's morals throughout the year. At the year's end he leaves to report to the Jade Emperor, the leading Taoist deity. But before he departs, the head of the household, in festive spirit, symbolically smears Tsao Chun's mouth with sweets or drugs him with wine. A sweetened mouth, like a bribed official, speaks no evil; a deity befuddled with liquor gets no imperial audience. Either way, the family can live in safety for one more year.

Not long after the time of Li Shao-chun, rural churches organized by faith healers who attracted vast peasant followings began to emerge as an element of Taoism. The Yellow

Turban and the Five Pecks of Rice bands became the best known of these organizations. Both groups practised mass emotional rites to cure illness and expiate sin. A variety of "inner hygiene" systems existed, and one called the Union of Vital Energy brought the Taoists many converts and much condemnation from the Confucianists.

The Union of Vital Energy was based on the idea that *Yang*, the male principle, and *Yin*, the female principle, nourished each other and could together be employed to promote longevity. The husbanding and direction of sexual energy constituted the key to longevity, and to believers it still does. The legendary Yellow Emperor, who was reputedly able to nourish 1,200 concubines, is still considered a model for longevity-seeking Taoists to emulate.

In A.D. 184 the two rural sects revolted against the Han Dynasty. Bloody fighting raged for more than three decades, but in the end Taoism as a military threat was finished. Later, however, Taoism enjoyed frequent periods of royal favour. Under both the T'ang and Sung Dynasties great monasteries and convents flourished. Taoist beliefs rooted themselves tenaciously in the soul of China, although no unified Taoist church ever emerged.

By the time the Communists took over in China, Taoism as a religion had for long been a spent force. Philosophical Taoism, heavily adulterated by superstition but perhaps also fortified by it, nevertheless retains a hold on millions. It serves as an element of passive resistance to a modern insistence on conformity more rigid than anything Confucius—or his adapters—ever dreamed of.

UNLIKE Taoism, which had originated in China, Buddhism entered as an immigrant faith with travellers from Central Asia. As a foreign religion it might never have taken root if China had been united and peaceful after its arrival. As it was, the old values of Confucian society were shattered during the four centuries of banditry and slaughter that followed the break-up of the Han Dynasty in the third century. In the chaos, people sought solace from new values. Some turned to Taoism, others to Buddhism, and some to both.

The basic tenets of Buddhism were something very new for China, and the novelty itself may have appealed to many. Buddhism's ultimate aim was to release the individual from reincarnation—the seemingly endless cycle of existence that is the core of the beliefs of Hinduism, the earlier Indian religion from which Buddhism derived. Hindus believed that when a person dies his soul is reborn into the world in another guise to bear all the temporal pains and pleasures of birth, life and death. The reincarnated being might exist as a lowly cockroach or a mighty king, depending on his *karma*, the accumulated total of deeds of his previous existence.

HINDUISM taught that the cycle was never-ending, but Buddhists believed that the repetitive suffering experienced in reincarnation after reincarnation could be avoided by the attainment of nirvana. Nirvana has been variously defined. Final union with the supreme soul of the universe was one intellectualized definition. Another, with wider appeal, was that nirvana is everlasting, indescribable peace, a state of eternal bliss.

Attainment of nirvana was not easy. An individual had to eliminate selfishness and all desire for earthly pleasures. That meant practising sexual abstinence, doing good deeds and spending years in endless contemplation. Obviously such a life was only for monks and nuns, not for the Chinese masses. But Buddhism developed some practical modifications to deal with that problem.

Since a person's status was the result of his *karma*, Buddists taught, like the Hindus before them, that an individual could improve his future lot by proper conduct in any given existence. In theory then, nirvana could be reached by stages. Men and women unable to retire to a cloister could take the first steps towards salvation by abstaining from taking life, lying, stealing, drinking liquor or engaging in adultery. Moreover, through Buddhism, it was also possible—by reciting from Buddhist scriptures and by performing charitable works—to assist ancestral spirits who might be suffering in the other world.

Thus, despite its alien Indian origins, Buddhism triumphed over the opposition of native Chinese Taoism and Confucianism. By the eighth century it had won millions of converts. It offered something for everyone. To the masses it gave hope of salvation, which could in some cases be attained by the simple process of repeating "O-mi-t'o-fu", the name of the compassionate Buddha. It appealed to intellectuals with its ethical doctrines and its interest in philosophical speculation. In the centuries that followed, numerous rulers became Buddhists, and its influence was widely felt in art, literature and philosophy.

Although Buddhism is no longer so vital a force as it once was, the religion still claims many followers. On Taiwan, Buddhist priests and laymen have become increasingly active in recent years. On the mainland, the Communists have organized the Buddhist Association. One of the Association's three honorary presidents, the Dalai Lama of Tibet, fled from the Communists in 1959, but the organization continues to direct effective propaganda at South-East Asian countries and claims to represent 100 million Buddhist believers. By elaborately restoring some well-known temples and by honouring an object believed to have been a tooth of the Buddha, the Communists have undoubtedly won some Buddhist supporters. They have also influenced many people with their promise to respect religious freedom.

THIS promise sounds fine to the naïve. Religiously inclined minority groups like the Tibetans and the Moslems, however, know how limited it is. *Nationalities Unity*, a journal for minority cadres, has openly warned that party members among the minorities who believe in religion and "think that religion and communism are not in opposition to each other [are] utterly mistaken".

China's Moslems are a very special problem for the Communists. Moslem traders first reached China around the middle of the seventh century, and probably 15 to 20 million Moslems now live in different parts of China. Most of them reside in the North-West provinces —Kansu, Chinghai and Sinkiang.

ALTHOUGH Moslem males are proud of their religious heritage, a number of them have taken non-Moslem Chinese wives. Nevertheless, integration into Chinese society has been slow, especially in the North-West, where the Chinese presence has been historically weak and where it is still resented. In 1958 alone, the Communists imprisoned some 7,000 Moslems in labour camps in the North-West because of their opposition to Communist agricultural and industrialization programmes.

The Chinese Communists themselves have officially acknowledged that there have been a number of Moslem risings in the North-West, and there have been others which they have kept quiet. Peking wants to maintain a favourable image in the Arab countries, and too much news of trouble with Moslems at home could be embarrassing. Complaints from Soviet Moslems along the Russian-Chinese border about mistreatment of their co-religionists have for long been an irritant in the Sino-Soviet quarrel. In 1959 and again in 1962 thousands of Moslems fled from China's Sinkiang province into Soviet Kazakhstan. Chinese Communist suspicion that the Russians sent some of these nomads back to China with guns was one of the reasons for China's closing of Russian consulates in the autumn of 1962.

Compared with Islam, Christianity has made a poor numerical showing in China. Christianity reached China almost simultaneously with Islam. But somehow, despite this early foothold, it never developed the staying power of Islam. Neither the ineffectual efforts of Roman Catholic missions during the Yuan Dynasty nor the more impressive exertions of 17th- and 18th-century Jesuits resulted in any large-scale conversions. By 1800, after more than 200 years of missionary work, there were perhaps 200,000 Chinese Catholics.

In the 1840s Western guns opened China to the merchant and missionary alike. For a century thousands of Catholics and Protestants laboured preaching the Gospel, running hospitals and building schools. The missionaries had great zeal, diplomatic backing and money. They were able to tempt the Chinese with offers of language instruction and technical education beneficial to them as individuals and useful to China as a country. Two of China's most prominent men, Sun Yat-sen and Chiang Kai-shek, became Christians and married American-educated Christians. Yet by 1949, the Roman Catholics could count only some 3.5 million converts and the Protestants only 900,000.

MEANWHILE a new ideology had arisen. Starting with only a handful of members in 1921, the Chinese Communist party by 1949 had grown to include a membership of almost 4.5 million. Today, with 19 million members, the party of Marx and Mao has far outstripped the churches of Christ in numbers of adherents. And, like the distressed Confucians who flocked to Buddhism in the turmoil accompanying the decline of the Han Dynasty, many of the best students from the missionary schools have transferred their allegiance from Christianity to Communism.

Christianity is however by no means finished in mainland China. Despite Communist persecution, there are still many devout Protestants and Roman Catholics. The inhabitants of a few North China villages, whose entire populations turned to Catholicism generations ago, have resisted all efforts to persuade them to abandon their "superstitions". But for the present, one fact is clear. Christianity, an alien doctrine with a long presence in China, has gained only a tenuous hold there. Communism, with only four decades in China and equally alien, seems to have struck a far more responsive chord in the modern Chinese mind than Christianity, Taoism, Buddhism or Confucianism. The fact is unpleasant—but undeniable.

A KITCHEN SHRINE is the dwelling of the household god who observes each family and reports on it yearly to the Jade Emperor. The divinity shown here is still universally worshipped.

A Hybrid of Magic and Metaphysics

The traditional religions of China are a peculiar intermingling of the foreign and the indigenous, the superstitious and the spiritual, the worldly and the other-worldly. A Buddhist male saint in transit from India is identified with a primitive Chinese fertility goddess; the two figures merge in China as the Goddess of Mercy, Kuan Yin. Lao Tzu, an ancient sage, preached mysticism and quietism; yet Taoism, a faith that purports to follow Lao Tzu, encompasses black magic, alchemy, elixirs of life, and hundreds of gods. Similarly, a man's passage into the other world is celebrated with the paraphernalia of this world: money, food and fireworks.

REVERENT WOMEN, Chinese living in Malaya, prepare bean cakes before an ancestor's grave. On a certain spring day, descendants burn paper money and offer food to the dead.

*RITUALS embellish
the polytheistic popular
religion that has
been absorbed by Taoism*

A DAZZLING THRONE, studded with blazing light bulbs (*left*), frames a priest who
leads an annual rite when seafaring families of Hong Kong pray for the drowned.

BURNING INCENSE offered by a priest
(*opposite*) rises in a cloud before two of the
large idols that surround the inner sanctuary of Peking's Temple of the Eastern Peak.

BLAZING CANDLES light the interior of a
small Peking temple (*below*). Many temples
were shut during 1966-7 as devoted Marxists sought to extend China's Revolution.

A BENIGN BUDDHA carved in about the fifth century A.D. still looks down from its richly painted niche. Tun-huang was a centre of Buddhist art and learning for more than 1,000 years.

CLIFFSIDE SHRINES contain numerous images of the Buddha and his disciples (*opposite*). The more than 450 shrines were restored and kept in repair by pious Buddhists for centuries.

88

sacred grottoes at Tun-huang, once a major stop on the pilgrimage route to India

6

Century of Humiliation

AMONG the most frequently quoted of China's ancient military thinkers is Sun Tzu, who lived in the sixth century B.C. This scholar's most famous maxim consists of only eight characters and can be translated:

Know your opponents; know yourself;
In a hundred battles, a hundred victories.

If the rulers of the declining Manchu Dynasty had paid more than lip service to this principle during the 19th and 20th centuries, the humiliations suffered by the Middle Kingdom during that period might well have been averted. But the Manchus were so convinced of the

inherent superiority of the Chinese way of life that they refused to acquire anything more than the most superficial knowledge about the West. That refusal left China virtually defenceless against 19th-century opponents who were more formidable than any the Chinese had ever encountered.

The complacent masters of East Asia were unaware that social and technological revolutions in Europe were producing traders and missionaries prepared to probe and settle the far corners of the world. By 1715, after nearly a century of sporadic trading efforts along the South China coast, the British had succeeded in establishing a base in Canton, where they were shortly joined by French, Dutch and American traders.

Canton was an unpleasant place in which to live or work. The Chinese authorities hampered trade with regulations that were often arbitrary. Foreign merchants were confined to a small enclave on the bank of the Pearl River and denied the company of women. They could not enter Canton proper, and were permitted to transact business only with merchants belonging to the *Co-hong*, a government-controlled monopoly. The foreigners were forbidden to communicate with government officials except through the *Co-hong*; to make matters worse, imperial regulations prohibited Chinese from teaching their language to foreigners.

NEITHER the Macartney mission to Peking in 1793 nor a delegation led by Lord Amherst in 1816 had any success in placing trade and diplomatic relations on what Europeans considered a normal basis. To the cultured officials of the Middle Kingdom, the pale-skinned strangers from the western seas rated treatment no different from that traditionally accorded more familiar "barbarians". If the Europeans, with their strange hair tints and outlandish clothes, were willing to observe the laws and customs of the only civilized country on earth, well and good. They could stay on the bank of the Pearl and exchange their goods and silver for Chinese tea, silks, rhubarb, lacquer and porcelain. But if they had any ideas about changing the way things had always been done in China, then they had better leave.

Accustomed to dealing with "natives" fearful of the white man's mechanical gadgets and firepower, the Canton traders considered the Chinese attitude intolerable. Even if the China trade had been confined solely to conventional goods, trouble would have come. But as the 18th century ended, a hitherto minor item of trade added a new dimension to the conflict between the West and China. That once minor item was the stuff dreams, fortunes and nightmares are made of—opium.

The Chinese had been familiar with opium long before Europeans started bringing it to China in bulk. Chinese medical books of the 13th and 14th centuries recommended the drug for diarrhoea and dysentery, but warned that, carelessly used, it "kills like a knife". When the first imperial decree against the sale and use of opium for non-medical purposes was issued in 1729, about 200 chests, each holding 120 to 160 pounds of raw opium, were being brought in annually to serve the needs of a constantly increasing number of addicts. Judging by their effectiveness, however, the 1729 edict and subsequent prohibitions served merely to underline the inability of the Manchu government to enforce the Emperor's will.

In the century following the first edict, imports of opium increased phenomenally. By 1831 the annual volume had reached nearly 19,000 chests, and vast amounts of Chinese silver were being expended to pay for them. All sorts of people—respectable British merchants, staid New England skippers, Chinese fishermen and provincial officials—became engaged in the increasingly lucrative trade. During the 1838-9 trade year some 30,000 chests were shipped from India to China; there would have been more had it not been for the appointment to Canton of an outstanding official named Lin Tse-hsu with orders to wipe out the traffic.

AS governor-general of Hunan and Hupeh provinces, Lin had distinguished himself by suppressing the traffic in Central China. In Canton he exacted obedience from the conniving citizens and officials by threatening to cut off the head of anyone who disobeyed his orders to surrender all opium. When the foreigners, who had heard many an empty decree, tried to stall, Lin pulled all Chinese employees out of the traders' enclave, ringed it with troops and cut off food supplies. Indignant but powerless, the foreign merchants surrendered about four million pounds' worth of opium—which Lin promptly and publicly destroyed.

The British firms in Canton were naturally outraged by Lin's act. Captain Charles Elliot, the chief British official in Canton, ordered all British subjects and ships to leave the city for the near-by Portuguese-held enclave of Macao. There the British carried on the opium trade with even more vigour, while other foreign traders continued their operations elsewhere along the coast. The stage was being set for still more serious trouble.

NEITHER the opium trade nor Lin Tse-hsu's attempt to suppress it were the sole reasons for what followed—the conflict now known as the Opium War. The basic dispute was both simpler and more complex. As a sovereign nation, China followed well-established customs and laws which it saw no reason to modify. The Western traders had their own customs and laws, which were vastly different from those of the Chinese and which they too were unwilling to alter. Ideally, the vendors of textiles, opium and Christianity should have respected China's sovereignty and permitted the country to pursue its own ways. But the Westerners, motivated both by the desire for profit and the wish to bring the benefits of the white man's civilization to the ignorant heathen, were not over concerned about sovereignty.

With disengagement and compromise impossible, both sides turned to force. Sporadic and indecisive clashes occurred throughout the winter of 1839-40. The next summer a British fleet made a foray up the coast from Hong Kong. It shelled Amoy and later took the city of Tinghai on Chusan, an island near Shanghai.

News of these defeats at the hands of barbarians enraged the Emperor, for solicitous underlings had led the august leader to believe that the invaders were being easily disposed of. With part of the unhappy truth out that the Middle Kingdom was virtually defenceless, and with the Celestial Throne demanding an explanation, a scapegoat had to be found. Self-seeking officials blamed Lin Tse-hsu and his get-tough policy for the catastrophe. The erstwhile hero was dismissed.

In disgrace, Lin risked his life by trying to advise the Emperor that China would have to

FOREIGN "FACTORIES", headquarters of European and American merchants along the Pearl River in Canton, are shown in a stylized painting made in the 19th century. In front of them on tall flagstaffs fly the flags of Britain, Holland and the United States, among others. Each factory served as the treasury, office and living quarters of the mercantile agent operating it.

modernize its defences by acquiring European-style ships and guns. Lin was exiled to the barren North-West, and his advice ignored. When fighting flared again in 1841 and 1842, the Chinese paid dearly for their stubborn ignorance. Peasant militia and Manchu regulars were able to inflict only a few local defeats on British troops. In the summer of 1842 the British rapidly overran Chinese defences at the mouth of the Yangtze. Moving up-river, they quickly took Shanghai and pushed on towards Nanking. With the city about to fall, the Manchus agreed to negotiate.

Earlier dynasties had occasionally bought off barbarians by sending them silks, horses and princesses. But never had any dynasty granted anything like the concessions the Manchus made to Britain and to the other Western powers which took advantage of China's weakness in the following two years. The island of Hong Kong was ceded to Britain in perpetuity. Five ports—Canton, Amoy, Foochow, Ningpo and Shanghai—were opened to trade and permission was granted for aliens to reside in them. Chinese courts in these treaty ports were denied jurisdiction over foreigners. In addition, the Manchus paid the British £7,500,000 in reparations. Ironically, there was no mention in any of the treaties of the opium traffic which had been the ostensible cause of the war.

Shocked and humiliated by defeat at the hands of the supposed inferiors, some scholar-officials sought to bolster China's defences by making use of foreign weapons and machinery. They also advocated utilizing the old border-region tactic of instigating fights between barbarian groups to the advantage of China. But all these lines of action required association with foreigners and the acquisition of knowledge alien to orthodox belief. Very few men of ability deigned or dared to be so radical. Some officials sought individual escape through the classics or opium. Others, especially in the South, encouraged popular agitation for resistance. Boastful placards were produced denouncing the British as "rebellious barbarian dogs and sheep", adding that "We are definitely going to kill you, cut your heads off and burn you to death!"

HAD the Manchu government been internally strong, China could have given the external enemy considerable difficulty. But even before the end of the 18th century, floods, famines, peasant rebellions and frontier wars had begun to plague the dynasty and sap its strength. By the middle of the 19th century brigands and anti-Manchu rebels were creating chaos in virtually every province.

The bloodiest and most important of these outbreaks, the T'ai P'ing rebellion, began in 1850. Hung Hsiu-ch'uan, leader of this revolt, was a Cantonese who had been influenced by some translated Christian pamphlets and an American missionary. During an illness, Hung experienced visions which convinced him that he was Christ's younger brother, chosen to restore the worship of the true God and to establish on earth a *T'ai P'ing T'ien Kuo*, or "Heavenly Kingdom of Great Peace".

Hung and his band of converts got into trouble by smashing idols in village temples in Kwangsi, and were chased into the near-by mountains by local troops. There, in classic rebel pattern, they armed and organized themselves. Hung preached a fundamentalist Christian doctrine mixed with varying shades of Confucianism. He prohibited prostitution, slavery, adultery, witchcraft, gambling, and the use of tobacco, alcohol or opium. Avowedly anti-Manchu and advocating agrarian reform and communal ownership, he soon attracted thousands of recruits. Moving north in 1852, the rebels swept through Hunan, gathering supporters and supplies *en route*. In March 1853 they stormed into Nanking and slaughtered the Manchu garrison.

For the next 11 years the T'ai P'ings held Nanking as their capital. Their forces fought almost to Peking, and seesaw battles with imperial troops turned much of the fertile Yangtze Valley into a terrorized wasteland. Rebel attacks on Shanghai led eventually to the creation of the "Ever-Victorious Army", a mixed force of Asian and Western mercenaries serving the Manchus.

Reorganized imperial forces retook Nanking in 1864. Hung Hsiu-ch'uan killed himself during the siege, and by 1866 the remnants of his followers had been driven into the mountains of South China. The rebellion was broken. But the 16 years of war, accompanied by epidemics and widespread starvation, had taken a terrible toll. It has been estimated that 20 million persons died during the T'ai P'ing troubles.

EVEN as the Manchus struggled with domestic rebellion they faced increased external pressure. The settlements made during the early 1840s had satisfied neither Chinese nationalists nor foreign imperialists, and fighting broke out again in 1856. In 1858 British, French, American and Russian negotiators, backed by some 30 gunboats and some 3,000 troops, forced imperial delegates in Tientsin to sign treaties granting still more concessions.

The Manchus held back from honouring these treaties, and in 1860 foreign troops destroyed Peking's Summer Palace. The Emperor then opened 11 more ports to trade and granted permission for traders and missionaries to attempt to garner profit and souls in the interior of China. The treaties also permitted foreign envoys to reside in Peking, established a customs service under foreign control, and legalized the importation of opium.

A FEW patriotic officials realized that China could not hope to preserve its own traditions and customs without making some effort to learn Western military and industrial methods. They had only limited success with their proposals for change. A few students were trained in Western languages and science. Some arsenals, shipyards and factories were built. But there was no broad effort to acquire Western techniques, as there was in neighbouring Japan.

After almost 20 years of rivalry in Korea, China and Japan went to war in 1894. The Japanese quickly crushed the Chinese. The 1895 Treaty of Shimonoseki forced China to recognize the independence of Korea. Taiwan, the Pescadores and part of Manchuria were ceded to Japan.

China swung from extremes of unrealistic hope to total despair in the concluding years of the 19th century. Reformers won the attention of the 27-year-old Emperor Kuang Hsu in 1898; during what came to be called the "One Hundred Days" of reform, Kuang Hsu ordered a sweeping modernization of the traditional system. The development of agriculture, industry and communications was to be encouraged; the school and civil-service systems were to be overhauled. These and dozens of other reforms were ordered but none was ever put into practice. With the support of conservative ministers whose positions and incomes would have been imperilled by the modernization, the ageing Empress Dowager Tz'u Hsi staged a *coup d'état*. She imprisoned her naïve nephew and annulled his decrees.

European powers in the interim capitalized on China's transparent weakness in a frenzied race for exclusive economic concessions. The French demanded and received extensive rights in Kwangtung, Kwangsi and Yunnan in the South; the Russians forced the granting of railway rights and port leases in Manchuria; the Germans acquired rail and mining concessions in Shantung; the British expanded their territorial holdings opposite Hong Kong and obtained developmental rights in the Yangtze Valley; and Japan demanded and received trading concessions in Fukien province.

Busy developing its own western lands, the United States made few special demands but did secure all the privileges China was granting to other countries. When the Western powers started scrambling for concessions, the U.S. Secretary of State, John Hay, became concerned over the possibility that China might be carved up into commercial protectorates. He successfully advocated a policy of equal sharing of all concessions. While the United States claimed to be motivated as much by the idealistic wish to safeguard the territorial integrity of China as by the desire to trade in China, Chinese often regard Hay's "Open Door" policy as an effort to ensure America's share in the loot of their country.

WHILE military defeats and territorial concessions were especially humiliating to imperial officials, foreign efforts to Christianize China did much to create mass antagonism. The vast majority of the Christian missionaries were dedicated tenders of bodily and spiritual ills, but many interfered in local lawsuits, customs and government, arousing the hostility of peasant and gentry alike. Simultaneously, anti-Manchu outbreaks increased. Seizing on anti-foreign feelings, imperial officials began tacitly encouraging the xenophobic activities of secret societies and associations. Chief among these was the I Ho Ch'uan, a North China group which came to be known as the "Boxers" because its members considered themselves invulnerable after performing ritual shadow-boxing exercises. By the summer of 1900, court officials had convinced the Empress Dowager that the Boxers should be given official support. The resulting "Boxer Rising" was a bloody fiasco. Attracting supporters and massacring

Christians as they moved north, the Boxers entered Peking in June 1900. There they besieged some 1,000 foreigners and 3,000 Chinese Christians in the hastily fortified Legation Quarter for 55 terrifying days. Superior firepower enabled the defenders to hold out until a seven-nation expeditionary force drove off the attackers. Casualties in the Legation Quarter were low, but in the rest of Peking and in the countryside thousands of converts were slain.

The foreign powers slapped the Manchu government with heavy penalties. In the heart of Peking a huge section was set aside for the use of foreign legations. No Chinese had the right to reside in this area, which was to be permanently garrisoned by foreign troops. In addition China agreed to pay 13 countries indemnities and interest amounting to £265 million. Some of these indemnities were later remitted or forgiven by a few of the Western powers, and several of the powers, following America's example, stipulated that their indemnities be used for the education of Chinese youths.

IN the meantime, blame for the accumulated humiliations fell mostly on the ruling Manchus. Alarmed, they made some efforts at reform. Convinced, however, that reform under the crafty old Empress Dowager was hopeless, many patriots turned to thoughts of revolution. Among the plotters was Sun Yat-sen, a 34-year-old doctor who was already a veteran conspirator at the time of the Boxer Rising.

The son of a Cantonese farmer, Sun had studied in China, Hawaii, Hong Kong, and the libraries of London—where his reading included the works of Henry George and Karl Marx. Despite his Western knowledge, he had enough Chinese education to make him acceptable in an essentially anti-foreign society. A Christian with useful foreign connections, Sun was also closely associated with anti-Manchu secret societies in the South.

During his revolutionary activity, Sun criss-crossed the globe, raising funds from overseas Chinese in South-East Asia, Hawaii, the United States and Europe. In China itself his followers launched one unsuccessful revolt after another. In 1911, when an accidental rising finally touched off the national revolution, Sun was raising funds about as far from the scene of action as possible—Denver, Colorado.

The rising, which took place at Wuchang on the Yangtze River on October 10, was no demonstration of expert planning or skilful military action. A bomb cached in a revolutionary headquarters accidentally exploded and aroused the suspicions of jittery Manchu officers. They arrested some suspects and obtained a revolutionary roster. In panic, revolutionaries in imperial artillery and engineering units attacked the headquarters of the imperial viceroy. The viceroy fled and tried to get foreign gunboats to shell the rebels. Influenced by the French consul, an old friend of Sun Yat-sen, the foreigners remained neutral, and the revolution, drawing strength from years of discontent, spread rapidly. When Sun Yat-sen reached Shanghai from abroad on December 24, 1911, most of the South was in revolt.

Sun was sworn in as first President of the Republic of China at the new capital of Nanking on January 1, 1912, but the realities of power politics cut his term to 43 days. With no experience of running even a county, and without an army to support him, Sun had to yield to the wishes of northerners who objected to the idea of a radical Cantonese intruding on their bailiwicks. Yuan Shih-k'ai, a powerful and skilful officer who had played a role in the peaceful abdication of P'u Yi, the Manchu Boy-Emperor, assumed the Presidency and moved the capital back to Peking. For the ensuing four years Yuan was China's recognized head and its most powerful leader, but he failed to bring the country unity or prosperity.

AS the vigour of the Manchu rulers had declined, the power of provincial administrators had increased. Governors and generals who had sided with the rebels had often done so in the hope of strengthening their already considerable local autonomy and bargaining power on the national scene—and their hopes were often realized. Instead of creating a strong central government, the revolution caused China to be broken up into a collection of satrapies under jealous war lords fighting and bargaining for power.

In 1912 Sun and his supporters reorganized their secret revolutionary society as the Kuomintang, or "National People's party", and in 1913 attempted to overthrow Yuan Shih-k'ai. The attempt ended in failure, and Sun was forced to flee to Japan. There he married Soong Ch'ing-ling, an American-educated Christian, and resumed his peripatetic life of political intrigue.

FOR a decade neither Sun nor his socialist-oriented Kuomintang exercised a strong influence on China. Meanwhile disunity and grinding poverty continued to plague the mock republic. While the war lords wrestled for power and foreign nations seized concession after concession, Sun flitted in and out of the country, fruitlessly attempting to win support for still another try at unifying the divided land.

The year 1922, however, marked a turning-point for Sun—and for China. Harried out of Canton by an unsympathetic war lord, Sun took refuge aboard a supporter's gunboat which was moored, for safety's sake, among the foreign warships anchored in the river off Canton. There he was joined by a loyal, ramrod-straight young officer named Chiang Kai-shek. The son of a middle-class Chekiang farmer and merchant, Chiang already held a distinguished military record. A graduate of the Shinbo Gokyo Military Academy in Tokyo, he had commanded a detachment in the 1911 revolution and served as a staff officer in the 1913 revolt. Aloof but shrewd, he made a deep impression on Sun during their weeks together aboard ship. From then on Chiang rapidly acquired positions of trust and opportunity; within a short time it was apparent that Chiang was a leading contender for future party leadership.

It was also in 1922 that Sun at last obtained outside support. During a series of winter meetings with Soviet emissaries he obtained promises of Russian money and weapons. It was this aid that enabled Chiang to launch the 1926-8 Northern Expedition (see Chapter 7) which reduced the war lords' power and finally brought the country a measure of unity.

Tragically, Sun died of cancer in 1925 before unification had become more than a dream. But he left behind a series of lectures which gave the Kuomintang a basis for attracting mass support. The K.M.T. canonized these lectures as Sun's "Three Principles of the People". Never precisely defined, these principles urged (1) nationalism, (2) democracy and (3) improvement of the people's livelihood by land redistribution and control of private enterprise.

In a country where self-seeking war lords and foreign gunboats mocked national aspirations, it seemed necessary to subordinate the unfamiliar concept of democracy to "temporary" K.M.T. dictatorship, euphemistically known as "political tutelage". Moreover, Sun's measures for improving the people's livelihood had to be toned down until the "enemy" was defeated.

MORE than a few enemies faced China and Chiang Kai-shek. His closeness to Sun and influence over K.M.T. officers trained at the party's Whampoa Military Academy near Canton—of which he had been named commander in 1924—made him the country's most powerful man. At first Westerners distrusted Chiang because of the collaboration between the Kuomintang and the Russians. Chiang changed that attitude by turning on the Communists in 1927. That same year, Chiang married Soong Ch'ing-ling's sister, Mei-ling, and became a Christian. His conversion and alliance with the Soong family, which boasted a Harvard-educated financier in Mei-ling's brother T. V. Soong, made Chiang and China's cause more acceptable to many influential businessmen and missionaries. At the same time the Nationalist government attracted many educated and patriotic young men. Enthusiasm ran high, and for a few years China seemed to be *en route* to stability.

But deep in the countryside insurgent Communist guerrillas built up bases of power and, calling for land redistribution, fomented trouble among the peasants. Across the Sea of Japan, Japanese militarists noted China's stirrings of progress with alarm. In 1931 they rigged an incident and moved in force into Manchuria. As Generalissimo of China's armies, Chiang began trading space for time. Without the means to face the Japanese in the field, he minimized open warfare with them and concentrated on the Communists in the Kiangsi-Hunan mountains.

BY 1936 Chiang had the Communists on the run, but his efforts were losing him the support of officers commanding forces in the north which had been pushed out of Manchuria by the Japanese. These officers wanted more action against the Japanese. When the Generalissimo visited their headquarters in Sian in 1936 to bring them into line, they imprisoned him. The price of Chiang's release was the formation of an anti-Japanese "United Front" of Communists and Nationalists which gave the Communists a new lease on life.

The Japanese launched a major campaign in 1937 and by early 1938 the Nationalist government was holed up in Chungking, deep in the mountains of Szechwan. By 1940, the Japanese held Nanking and all the coastal cities. Unable to wield control over the vast hinterlands of China, the Japanese settled in for a war of attrition. In this period, neither the Communists nor the Nationalists fought the Japanese as vigorously as their propagandists led the world to believe, although there were heroic exceptions. After the U.S.A. entered World War II in 1941, both Communists and Nationalists avoided seeking combat with the Japanese. In the Chinese view, the Americans could fight the Japanese while they themselves prepared for the more important contest of who would rule China. Inevitably, however, the United States became deeply involved in that struggle too.

American combat advisers like General Joseph Stilwell, who came to despise Chiang, and amateur soldier-diplomats like General Patrick J. Hurley, who once avowed that Mao was no Communist, never fully understood the thinking underlying Nationalist-Communist military and diplomatic behaviour. Neither did some professional foreign service officers, who became disgusted at the hypocrisy and corruption among the Nationalists. But they and military intelligence analysts warned that civil war threatened when Japan surrendered. The military analysts also warned in 1945 that Mao and his disciplined followers were dedicated revolutionary Marxists—and likely to win in an armed showdown with Chiang's numerically superior forces.

Throughout 1945, American diplomats tried to arrange a settlement between Mao and Chiang in Chungking. Those efforts failed, and the predicted civil war ensued. For four years the United States alternately supported Chiang and attempted to bring about a coalition government. The enormity of the task defeated the best efforts of generals like Albert C. Wedemeyer and George C. Marshall, as well as of China-raised Ambassador John Leighton Stuart. By the end of 1949 the anticipated end had been all but realized, and Chiang had been forced to take refuge on Taiwan. And while shocked Americans entered the 1950s demanding to know how China had been lost, one of the men who knew best quietly put a large share of the blame where it most belonged.

IN a 1950 speech to Kuomintang officials, Chiang Kai-shek declared: "The disastrous military reverse on the mainland was not due to the overwhelming strength of the Communists, which was not strong enough to defeat our Revolutionary Army, but due to the organizational collapse, loose discipline, and low spirit of the party." The Kuomintang had also failed, Chiang declared, because it had "failed to enforce the Principle of the People's Livelihood". Victory over Japan had ended imperialism in China, but the inability to bring a measure of prosperity to China's people, a problem unsolved since Sun Yat-sen first mentioned it more than four decades earlier, had brought about the near-ruin of Sun's Kuomintang.

A YOUTHFUL LEADER, Chiang Kai-shek is shown (*right*) facing Sun Yat-sen (*left*) in a composite photograph made in 1923. Chiang was an officer on Dr. Sun's staff.

THE FIRST PRESIDENT of China, Dr. Sun Yat-sen stands beside his second wife, Soong Ch'ing-ling, now a Vice-Chairman of the Chinese People's Republic.

Discord Within, Usurpation from Without

The history of China in the first half of the 20th century is marked by bloody factionalism and unbridled passion. Many Chinese put the blame on the tottering Manchu Dynasty for their humiliating losses of land and rights to foreigners. Yet when the emperors departed, a new period of chaotic politics was inaugurated. For a while the magnetic personality and high ideals of Sun Yat-sen seemed to promise eventual unity and peace in China. But after his death in 1925 the Nationalists and the Communists, the two leading factions which Sun had brought into brief accord, broke apart and started on a long struggle for dominance which ended only in 1949 with the establishment of Communist hegemony over the mainland. Sun's dream of a free, powerful and democratic China seems to have vanished. And as long as economic difficulties remain, China will continue to be a troubled—and troubling—nation.

A HUMILIATING DEFEAT for a once proud China came in 1895 at the hands of the Japanese (*above*). The conflict forced China to cede Taiwan, the Pescadores and part of Manchuria to Japan.

THE BITTER RISING in 1900 led by fanatical "Boxers" opposing foreigners was crushed by Japanese, European and American troops (*below*). China had to pay indemnities to 13 countries.

CIVIL WAR flared in 1927 when Chiang Kai-shek turned on his Communist allies. The Reds withdrew to the mountains (*above*) where Nationalists (*left*) attacked them by land and air.

OPEN AGGRESSION by the Japanese began in 1937. By 1938 the enemy held the capital, Nanking (*below*). The threat led to a short-lived agreement between Communists and Nationalists.

THE COMMUNISTS, driven to the hills by the Nationalists, gradually built up their strength and discipline

DETERMINED LEADERS, Mao Tse-tung (*left*) and General Chu Teh (*right*) stand near their headquarters in Yenan. Both men felt peasants should be the backbone of the revolution.

A CAVE HOSPITAL in Shensi cares for Communist soldiers and civilians. An American, Dr. George Hatem, received £2 17s. 6d. a month for treating patients.

FIRST GRADUATES of the Communists' military academy in Yenan in 1937 listen to their president, Lin Piao. Lin, like others who joined the Long March, is now a party leader.

A PRIMITIVE DORMITORY houses girls of the Lu Hsun Academy in Shensi (*below*). Although living in dire hardship, students saw Marxism as a cure for China's ills.

AN OBJECT-LESSON in politics is discussed by cadets of the military academy. The writing and the map on the board illustrate the Japanese seizure of Manchuria on September 18, 1931.

LAST HOPES for a truce were blasted as the Communists swept to victory

A FRIENDLY TOAST between Mao Tse-tung (*left*) and Chiang Kai-shek (*right*) at a carefully arranged meeting in 1945 celebrates the beginning of Nationalist-Communist negotiations, which proved to be useless.

THE U.S. MEDIATOR, General George Marshall arrives in Yenan (*below*) to seek a truce with Chiang and Red leaders Chou En-lai (*far left*) Mao Tse-tung (*far right*) and Chu Teh (*centre*). In 1946 the truce collapsed.

DEFEATED NATIONALISTS are rounded up by Communist guards in 1946. While troops from Russia drove the Japanese out of Manchuria, Mao's guerrillas obtained abandoned Japanese weapons and turned them against Chiang. By 1948 the Communists controlled Manchuria.

PANICKED CITIZENS, swarming into Shanghai in April 1949, escape the advancing Communist army. In May, Shanghai surrendered without a fight. By the end of the year Chiang was forced to surrender his last mainland stronghold and remove the government to Taiwan.

Triumphant Communists enter Peking in January 1949, the ranks of soldiers led by a truckload of revolutionaries. Many foreigners

had fled, abandoning their property, like the Ford on the right.

7

The Road to Power

OCCASIONALLY, important world figures set out on historic courses of action at almost precisely the same time. This happened with Mao Tse-tung and Chiang Kai-shek in the early part of December 1949, when both men embarked on trips which marked significant stages in their careers. Almost as if underlining their bitter differences of more than two decades, these two leaders travelled in different directions, by different means of transport, and under starkly contrasting circumstances. The events leading up to these December travels help to explain why Mao Tse-tung, as head of Communist China, has considered himself not only equal but superior to Russia's rulers as the leader of world Communism.

Chiang Kai-shek began his trip at an airfield near Chengtu in the mountains of west China early in the afternoon of December 10. As a staff car carried the long-gowned figure to his American transport plane, explosions echoed in the distance; enemy troops were dangerously close. Chiang, his once powerful military forces all but destroyed in four years of civil war, boarded the aircraft and left the soil of mainland China. After seven hours' flying south and east over Communist-controlled territory, the plane landed on the island of Taiwan, Chiang's final refuge.

The details of Mao Tse-tung's trip are less clear. Presumably for security reasons, the Communists made no announcement of his departure from Peking. His line of travel was north to the Manchurian border and west by rail across Asia to Moscow, where he arrived at the Yaroslavl Station late in the afternoon of December 16.

Chiang made his flight to Taiwan, an island then possessing fewer than 10 million inhabitants, as a defeated, unwanted refugee. Mao made his trip as the triumphant leader of the most populous country in the world. He was prepared to stand up to Joseph Stalin, the absolute dictator of international Communism, and argue that his nation should rank as an equal partner in the apparently expanding Communist world. Previously, all Communist leaders had kowtowed to Stalin or been ostracized; with Mao, things were going to be different.

THE circumstances of those trips at the end of 1949 reflected a remarkable reversal of fortunes. Fifteen years earlier Mao, virtually unknown outside Communist circles, had been the head of a ragged guerrilla force. Chiang Kai-shek, as the recognized leader of China, was confidently predicting the end of the Communist "bandit" menace. What caused the turnabout?

It helps to understand Mao's triumph in 1949 and his influence in world politics thereafter if one remembers two facts: first, Mao early acquired an exceptionally deep understanding of the Chinese peasant; second, Mao's experience and education equipped him remarkably well for the ruthless struggle for the domination of China in the 20th century.

Mao Tse-tung was born to a peasant family in the village of Shaoshan in Hunan province on December 26, 1893. He was a first son, and his birth was an important event to Mao's tough, ex-soldier father. Filial pride apart, within a few years this son would become an unpaid unit of labour. There was nothing Marxist in the elder Mao's idea; it was a part of peasant life in China.

ACCORDING to the account Mao gave to the American writer Edgar Snow in 1936—which may be coloured by the fact that Mao's father was clearly not the kindest of men, nor his son the most amenable of boys—it did not take his father long to start getting back his investment on his first son. The father had the boy working at the age of six as he fought his way up from poor peasant status, scrimping and haggling over every bit of grain or copper coin. By the time Mao was 10, the senior Mao had accumulated 2.5 acres of land, and by the time the son was 13, the family holdings had been increased to 3.5 acres. Mao's father was a rich peasant, able to buy poorer men's grain cheaply, transport it to city markets, and extend mortgage credit. Careful investments, hard work and stringent denial—Mao claims that he and his younger brother never got meat or eggs to eat—had paid off.

While the psychological interpretation of history can easily be over-emphasized, there is little doubt that Mao Tse-tung's childhood and his relationship with his father had a strong effect on the future leader's outlook. Mao began to struggle and to hate at an early age. At first he lived in fear of his father, who beat him frequently. Then, as he told Snow, "I learned to hate him."

Mao also hated the hard farm work and niggardly diet. At first he also hated the local primary school where his father intended him to get just enough education to read and keep simple accounts. He shortly modified his view of the school. Literacy, acquired through the drudgery of memorizing the classics, opened up the inspiring delights of blood-and-thunder historical fiction (see Chapter 4). Moreover, knowledge of Confucius and Mencius proved useful; sometimes in heated arguments with his father, the boy managed to escape a beating by quoting an appropriate passage from the sages about the obligations of parents to children.

About this time in young Mao's life famine touched off a mob attack on the provincial governor's office in Changsha, some 40 miles away. Government troops whacked off the heads of the riot leaders and displayed them for would-be rebels to see. The following year, poor villagers seized a consignment of Mao family rice during a spring food shortage. Young Mao, becoming increasingly interested in contemporary affairs as his education and reading progressed, thought the action was wrong, but he felt no sympathy for his father's boundless wrath. The loss was just another minor incident in a country burdened with far more important problems.

With the help of family friends who persuaded his unwilling father that advanced education might increase his earning power, Mao Tse-tung left Shaoshan in 1909 with the vague conviction that modern education might help to save his ailing country. He spent the next decade studying in the classroom, in the library and—literally—in the field.

As a student, Mao concentrated on history and literature. He soon acquired a reputation as an excellent essayist, skilled at using historical allusion. He also became familiar with the elements of poetry, an art in which he demonstrated no great skill until much later.

AT one time convinced that a reformed monarchy was China's best hope, Mao switched into anti-Manchu revolutionary action in the summer of 1911 when he joined other youths in cutting off queues, the Manchu-style pigtails which the dynasty had forced Chinese to wear in token of loyalty to the régime. After the October 10 rising which eventually led to the overthrow of the Manchus, Mao spent six disillusioning months in an army unit before resuming his education. During World War I, Mao became deeply involved in radical student movements. In

MAO TSE-TUNG, POETIC REVOLUTIONARY

Like many revolutionary leaders, Mao Tse-tung has been a prolific writer. His most famous piece of prose apart from his aphoristic *Thoughts* is an explanation of the guerrilla tactics he followed during his years of struggle. It goes as follows: "The enemy advances, we retreat. The enemy halts, we harass. The enemy tires, we attack. The enemy retreats, we pursue." As a poet, Mao is considered by critics to be well above average. Here are four of his efforts.

LOUSHAN

Cold is the west wind;
Far in the frosty air the wild geese call in the
*   morning moonlight*
In the morning moonlight
The clatter of horses' hooves rings sharp,
And the bugle's note is muted.

Do not say that the strong pass is guarded with iron.
This very day in one step we shall pass its summit,
We shall pass its summit!
There the hills are blue like the sea,
And the dying sun like blood.

CHINGKANGSHAN

Below the hill were our flags and banners,
To the hilltop sounded our bugles and drums.
The foe surrounded us thousands strong,
But we were steadfast and never moved.

Our defence was strong as a wall,
Now did our wills unite like a fortress.
From Huangyangchieh came the thunder of guns,
And the enemy army had fled in the night!

HUICHANG

Soon the dawn will break in the east,
But do not say we are marching early;
Though we've travelled all over these green hills
*   we are not old yet,*
And the landscape here is beyond compare.

Straight from the wall of Huichang lofty peaks,
Range after range extend to the eastern ocean.
Our soldiers, pointing, gaze south towards Kwantung,
So green, so luxuriant in the distance.

YELLOW CRANE TOWER

Wide, wide through the mist of the land flow
*   the nine tributaries,*
Deeply, deeply scored is the line from north to south.
Blurred in the blue haze of the mist and the rain
The Snake and Tortoise Hills stand over the water.

The yellow crane has departed, who knows whither?
Only this travellers' resting-place remains.
With wine I drink a pledge to the surging torrent;
The tide of my heart rises high as its waves!

1919, when the news reached China that its delegates at the Paris Peace Conference had failed to prevent the assignment of Germany's pre-war holdings in China to Japan, mass anti-government meetings were held in many parts of the country. In Hunan, Mao Tse-tung led student agitation against Chang Ching-yao, the local war lord, and established a revolutionary magazine. Chang crushed both agitation and magazine. But Mao's anti-imperialist —although not yet Communist—views won him considerable prominence among young intellectuals.

Mao's conversion to Marxism began in Peking in 1920, when he read a Chinese translation of the *Communist Manifesto*. Peking, where every yellow-roofed palace or blood-red wall evokes centuries of proud history, was in those days a centre of intellectual ferment. Its university faculty was one of the best in the world. Mao, working in the university library, was able to attend lectures as an auditor. He read voraciously, listened, argued and moved steadily leftwards in his thinking.

BY the autumn of 1920 Mao was back in Hunan, teaching and indoctrinating students in Marxism. His formal tie with the Communist movement dates from the early summer of 1921, when he went to Shanghai for secret meetings which consolidated several Marxist groups into the Chinese Communist party. *En route* he confided to an old classmate, "If we work hard, in about thirty to fifty years' time the Communist party may be able to rule China."

During the next decade and a half, Mao became involved in a fantastic struggle for survival and power. It was a period of strange alliances, shifting allegiances and downright treachery. An outsider often found it difficult to distinguish between the timeless intrigues of Asian war lords and the manoeuvres of men who blithely quoted authorities as diverse as Thomas Jefferson and V. I. Lenin to justify their policies.

While the amateur Mao was acquiring revolutionary theory and experience, Lenin and his agents were seeking collaborators in China. Sun Yat-sen was an early and obvious candidate. By 1920 Soviet agents were working in Peking and Shanghai, organizing study groups and spotting able young men for future training. Hendricus Sneevliet, a Dutch Communist who had been present at the founding sessions of the Chinese party in 1921, visited Sun Yat-sen in the South that same year to make the first proposal for co-operation between the Russian Communist party and Sun's Kuomintang (K.M.T.).

UNDER the Sino-Russian agreement of 1923, Sun received substantial military assistance. He also obtained Russian agreement to a statement that "the conditions necessary for the establishment of either Communism or Socialism do not exist in China", an apparent assurance against a Soviet takeover. In return, the Russians received permission for members of the Chinese Communist party (C.C.P.) to join the Kuomintang. Under this arrangement Mao Tsetung, a member of the C.C.P. Central Committee, also joined the K.M.T. and became an alternate member of its Central Executive Committee.

In the years 1923-7, Mao shuttled from Canton to Changsha to Shanghai and back again. He worked at co-ordinating C.C.P.-K.M.T. activities; edited the *Political Daily*, an organ of the K.M.T. political department; served as head of the K.M.T. propaganda committee; and trained cadres from all over the country in organizational techniques.

The surprising thing about this multi-faceted collaboration among Chinese and Russians, Nationalists and Communists, is that it lasted as long as it did. Dissension and distrust were everywhere. Militant Communists denounced those who co-operated with the Nationalists in obedience to Stalin's wishes. Right-wing Nationalists distrusted everyone, including members of their own cliques. Even the Russians quarrelled among themselves. Arguments raged on every level—personal, national, regional and political. But despite the death of Sun Yat-sen in 1925, this uneasiest of alliances functioned remarkably well until the launching of the

Northern Expedition that brought Chiang Kai-shek to power in 1927.

As commandant of the Russian-modelled Whampoa Military Academy in Canton, Chiang had emerged, with the support of the Whampoa cadets and officers, as the strongest man in the Kuomintang after Sun's death. He was dedicated to Sun's ideals of national unity and freedom from foreign domination. He was also a consummate juggler of factions with no compunctions about using Communist techniques and Communist personnel to consolidate his own power and to defeat the regional war lords who had kept the country divided and weak.

The Northern Expedition, with Chiang Kai-shek as Commander-in-Chief, started from Canton in the summer of 1926. Chiang's Whampoa cadets were the disciplined shock troops. In the countryside Mao Tse-tung and other organizers, preaching land reform and revolt, swung millions of peasants against the war lords. In Shanghai, Hankow and other cities, underground workers like Liu Shao-ch'i and Chou En-lai rallied the workers and intellectuals to the Nationalist cause. The Communist-directed underground in Shanghai was especially helpful in delivering the city to Chiang in the spring of 1927. But this support for Chiang did not mean that the Communists were his whole-hearted admirers. If the Communists had succeeded in gaining control of the country at that time, Chiang's usefulness as a military man might have allowed him a position in the Communist scheme of things; it is more likely that he would have been eliminated.

BUT Chiang Kai-shek was no stranger either to Shanghai or intrigue. He had established some underground connections of his own in the city, and he used them well. At 4.00 a.m. on April 12, 1927, a bugle blast and a ship's siren rent the air. Machine-guns opened up all over the great sprawling city, and the "counter-revolution" was on. Nobody knows how many thousands of Communists and their left-wing supporters died in bloody pitched battles, in front of firing squads or in torture

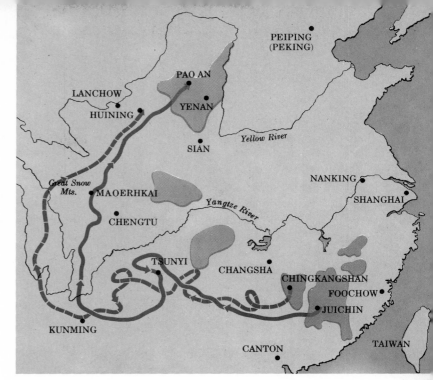

THE LONG MARCH began in October 1934 when the Communists, their forces encircled (*areas in colour above*), decided to break out. Fleeing to the west in a main force (*solid line*), an auxiliary body (*dotted line*), and other groups, they withstood countless attacks and ended up 6,000 miles away and 12 months later in the north, eventually establishing their capital at Yenan.

chambers during the months that followed. For the Chinese Communists and the Soviet agents it was a disastrous blow. Before the *coup* C.C.P. membership had been more than 50,000; when pressure had let up sufficiently for the party to check its membership rolls, only about 10,000 survivors were able, or willing, to be counted.

When Chiang launched his anti-Communist purge, Mao Tse-tung had been in the interior of China, working out some power-grabbing ideas of his own. He had been awed by the explosive forces generated when peasant associations in Kwangtung, Hunan and Hupeh recruited two million farmers and set them against landowners and war lords opposing the Northern Expedition, and he was determined to exploit this volatile reservoir of revolutionary manpower. He published an impassioned report in which he insisted that any successful Chinese revolution would have to be based on the peasantry.

This rank heresy, denying to the urban proletariat the supreme revolutionary role assigned to it by orthodox Marxist theory, later plunged

111

Mao into an ideological battle not only with Stalin and his agents in China but also with the men who then held the most senior posts in the C.C.P. Mao's report is now a classic of Chinese Communist literature. "The force of the peasantry," he wrote, "is like the raging winds and driving rains. It is rapidly increasing in violence. No force can stand in its way." Declaring that the peasants, "with their rough, blackened hands", would inevitably move into the forefront in China's revolution, he asked: "Shall we stand in the vanguard and lead them or stand behind and oppose them? . . . destiny will force us to pick an answer soon. . . ."

MAO's own peasant background, combined with his insight into the potentiality of Marxism for manipulating the forces of peasant discontent and traditional nationalism, made him a rare type among Chinese revolutionaries. But Mao faced formidable opposition from orthodox Marxists and other experienced and equally ruthless politicians. None the less, in time Mao outmanoeuvred, eliminated or won over most of his opponents. He disregarded the Russian agents, and so tenuous was his tie with the Kremlin in the early 1930s that a Soviet bulletin once printed his obituary.

Mao began his actual rise to the top of the Communist hierarchy at Chingkangshan, a small village in the mountains straddling the borders of Hunan and Kiangsi. After the failure of a peasant rising in Hunan had caused his dismissal from the party's Politburo, he had escaped into the hills with some 1,000 survivors. He was joined there late in 1927 by the forces of two bandit leaders. Then, in the spring of 1928, Chu Teh, a vigorous professional officer who had joined the Communist party in Germany, led about 2,000 men to Chingkangshan. From then until 1933 Mao was increasingly successful in his efforts to consolidate his own power in the party and to build up a Red Army capable of seizing and holding independent revolutionary bases. In that period, party membership climbed from 40,000 to 300,000; the number of Red Army rifles increased from around a thousand to perhaps 100,000.

The gradual build-up of Communist power did not escape Chiang Kai-shek's attention. Alert to the threat of armed, self-sufficient revolutionary bases, Chiang began his first "bandit extermination campaign" in December 1930. That campaign, and three which followed, failed to dislodge the Communists. In the fifth campaign, in October 1933, 400,000 Nationalist troops killed a probable 60,000 Red Army soldiers, and as many as a million peasants in the area may have died of starvation or been slaughtered as a result of the fighting. The Communists, seeing that they could not hold out against such massive attacks, decided to pull out. This brought about the famous "Long March".

Taking more than a year to complete, the 6,000-mile Long March was an epic of human perseverance. Approximately 90,000 troops started out late in 1934; perhaps 20,000 fought their way to Pao An in Shensi province, where Mao set up a temporary headquarters. In December 1936 he established a permanent base at Yenan. The journey was no ordinary forced march, but a series of running battles, fought while the marchers were moving across 18 mountain ranges and 24 rivers. It is small wonder that those who participated in that saga and still survive—and this includes the core of the Politburo which rules China today—for long maintained a unity found in no other Communist régime.

BETWEEN 1938 and 1941 the Russians, mindful of the Japanese presence of their eastern flank, sent £90 million worth of planes, guns and ammunition to Chiang Kai-shek's government. The Chinese Communists received only a tiny portion of this aid since their forces had technically been integrated into the Nationalist Army under the anti-Japanese "United Front" agreement forced on Chiang by the Manchurian officers who had kidnapped him in 1936 (see Chapter 6). But the United Front did give the Communists breathing-space to consolidate their positions in the "liberated" areas of the North-West, and to carry out propaganda work among Chinese and foreigners in the Nationalist areas. The effectiveness with which the Communists did these jobs, plus their deep infiltration of Japanese-occupied areas, contributed both to their prestige and their actual strength towards the end of World War II.

By that time their power was considerable. In 1944 the U.S. War Department commissioned a study of the Chinese Communist movement. Delivered in July 1945, but classified secret until August 1949, the report was a remarkably sober and accurate one. It made two blunt points: "The Chinese Communists *are* Communists," and "They are the most effectively organized group in China." While acknowledging the importance of Communist agrarian policy, the report convincingly showed that the Chinese Communists had never been and never would be simply "agrarian reformers". Revolution, culminating in a Communist state, was their clearly stated goal. Terming the C.C.P. "the best led and most vigorous" organization in China, the report said the Communists "enjoy wider popular support in the areas held by their armies than do the Nationalists in their areas of control". The "present trend" was "definitely in favour of the Communists".

EVENTS in the next four years confirmed the accuracy of this analysis. The loose discipline, corruption and low spirit clearly observable among Nationalist officials between 1945 and 1949 led finally to victory for Mao Tse-tung and the C.C.P. Communist troops entered Peking in January 1949, and by the end of the year they had routed the Nationalists in most of the rest of China.

The Communist victory had not come about as the result of any remarkable plots or betrayals. The people of China were tired and disillusioned after more than eight years of war. The Nationalists under Chiang had begun with a 4 to 1 superiority in weapons and men, but neither their promises nor their occasional concrete achievements could compete effectively with those of the well-organized, devoted

Communists. Both sides lied and cheated, but the Communists lied more convincingly, cheated less obviously and fought more effectively than the Nationalists.

Despite Stalin's insistence on K.M.T.-C.C.P. collaboration in the 1920s, despite his lack of help to the C.C.P. in the 1930s and early 1940s, and despite his advice in 1945 that Mao should not try to fight an all-out war against Chiang Kai-shek, Mao Tse-tung had emerged victorious. Fully aware that his country needed Russia's economic assistance, Mao set out on that December 1949 journey determined to make the most of China's new status.

Mao demonstrated on that first trip that his victory had been no fluke. When he arrived in Moscow he was expected to stay only a short time. It was assumed that he would pledge loyalty to Stalin and, in exchange for economic and military assistance, grant extensive concessions to the Russians in China.

But Mao's visit stretched to two months; he did voice thanks to Stalin as "teacher and friend of the Chinese people", but he was not obsequious in his praise. When formal agreements were finally announced early in 1950, China had indeed granted Russia major concessions in Manchuria and in other areas along the Sino-Soviet border. But the concessions were only short-term ones, and they bore indications of hard bargaining. Soviet economic assistance was limited to a five-year, £107 million loan, although Mao did get a military agreement promising him Soviet intervention if China should fight either Japan "or any state allied with it".

TO get the help that China badly needed for reconstruction, Mao Tse-tung reluctantly agreed in Moscow to deals that put him in Stalin's debt, and in the early years of his régime Soviet aid was of considerable value to Communist China. But none of it was to make Mao grateful; within a decade the peasant boy from Hunan province would be in open, angry conflict with the men who succeeded to Joseph Stalin's power in Russia.

A REVOLUTIONARY ZEALOT, Mao Tse-tung's fourth wife, who goes by the name of Chiang Ching, addresses a Red Guard rally. A former film actress, she has become an important and rabid leader of the Cultural Revolution.

REVOLUTIONARY LEADERS, Mao and the Defence Minister Lin Piao clap in response to Red Guard cheers. Lin appears to have been Mao's chief ally in launching the Cultural Revolution, keeping the army in hand.

REVOLUTIONARY YOUTHS, Red Guards with flags and arm bands demonstrate in Peking's T'ien An Men Square. The Red Guard was formed in August, 1966, and quickly became a fanatically pro-Mao weapon in the struggle sweeping China.

Red China Convulsed by a Vast Upheaval

Mao Tse-tung and his fellow veteran Communist leaders ruled a relatively stable and unified China for almost two decades after their victory in 1949. Then, suddenly, the ancient land, so often rent with strife before, was plunged into a maelstrom of political discord triggered by Communist Party Chairman Mao himself. Apparently convinced that the party had become too bureaucratic and that the nation had lost its revolutionary

zeal, Mao in 1966 launched a "Great Proletarian Cultural Revolution". Forming the country's youth into a fanatical Red Guard pledged to root out any anti-Mao or pro-Western thought, he also attacked even such old Comrades as Liu Shao-ch'i, China's President, who disagreed with his policy. The result was widespread chaos as various factions battled for power and whole provinces seemed on the verge of revolt.

ENORMOUS POSTERS made of newspapers and covered by Chinese Big Character writing give the latest news of the Cultural Revolution. The Red Guard plastered such posters on thousands of China's ancient walls, or spread them on the streets. Many posters attacked local and national officials for anti-Mao behaviour and "revisionism"—that is, favouring Russia's less exacting form of Marxism to China's. Many of the officials attacked were forced from office.

MARCHING MAOISTS, a red guard unit straggles down a road near the city of Hangchow. Bands of red guards roamed the countryside, especially in September-November, 1966, often terrorizing "bourgeois" merchants and provoking riots.

UNIFORMED TROOPS of China's 2.7 million-man People's Liberation Army stride through Canton wearing antiseptic face masks. The army appeared to be a force for moderation and cohesion through the cultural revolution's early chaotic stages.

DISGRACED OFFICIALS, forced to wear dunce caps and signs proclaiming their "crimes", are paraded through the streets in a truck by red guards. Many of China's leading artists and intellectuals were treated in a similar way.

A DAY NURSERY in an urban commune shelters infants playing below a portrait of Mao Tse-tung. The nurseries, set up in 1949, free mothers to work in industry and other enterprises.

YOUNG ENGINEERS pore over textbooks at the Shanghai University of Science and Technology. Despite technical emphasis, China failed to meet a goal of 2 million engineers by 1967.

A LANGUAGE CHART with simplified Chinese characters and their Latinized spelling is employed by students. Romanization of the language is not popular but the new characters are.

为 了 适 应
Weiliao shiying

发 展 为 经 济 建
fazhan wei jingji jian

各 是：扫 除 文
hi saochu wen

字 的 创 制
zi de chuangzhi

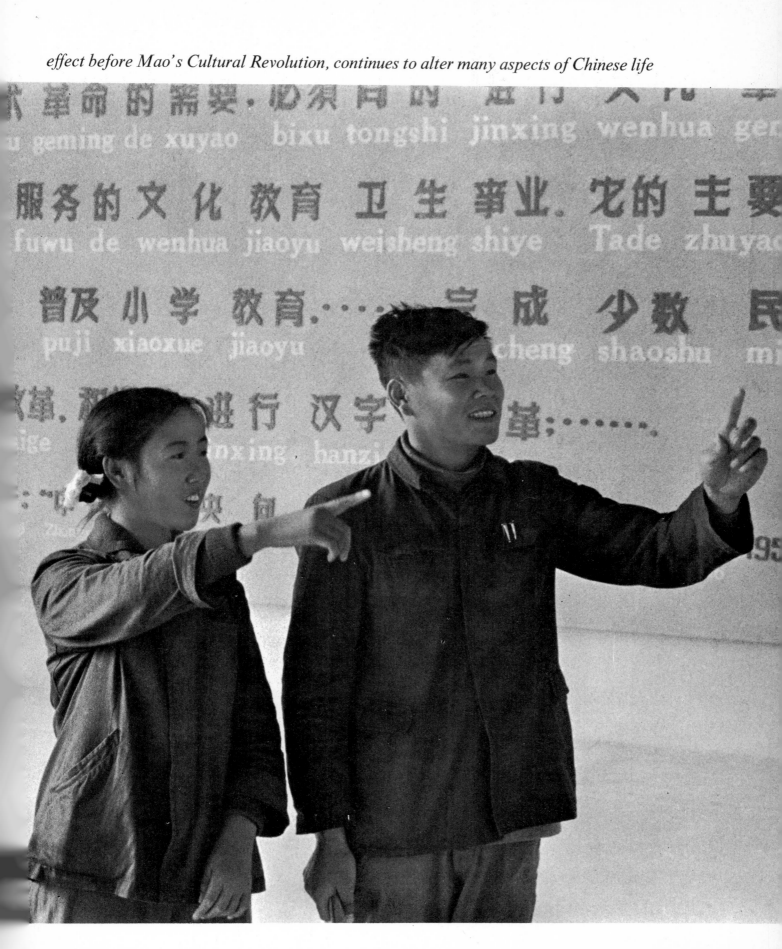

Steelworkers, some of them still wearing protective caps or helmets, eat in the employees' cafeteria of a steelmill near Peking. Hanging from

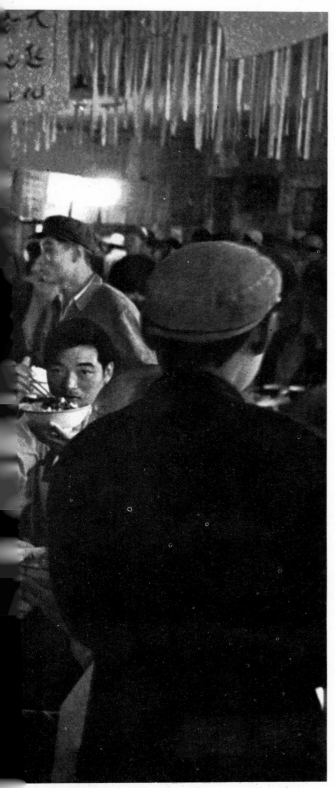

8

Under Communist Rule

WHAT is life like in the People's Republic of China? How have the Communists turned this once enfeebled and corrupt country, ruled by squabbling warlords, into a seemingly powerful nation capable of worrying much of the rest of the world with belligerent threats?

The answer to the first question is relatively simple. Life, as it almost always has been for most of the Chinese, is grim. Food is generally adequate, but scarcities persist. The individual is unimportant and the state supreme.

The answer to the second question is much more complicated. But a large measure of the Communists' initial success has been due to their ability to ensure that the limited material goods of this grim life—food, clothing and shelter—are shared on a roughly equitable basis.

People in the affluent countries of the West may scoff at the idea that shared poverty can be a political asset. But in a country where in times past drought, famine and flood often left the countryside reeking with the stench of

above are some of the ubiquitous signs urging higher production.

corpses, the ability to prevent mass starvation has been crucially important. Rice and wheat for the belly and protection from the elements are more important in Asia than are Western concepts of political freedom, which most of China's population has never known.

Furthermore, the power to carry out decrees or slogans and to fulfil threats and promises has traditionally created respect in China. In Chinese the term for the Communist party, *Kungch'antang*, is itself a slogan and a promise. Literally rendered, *kung* means "share", *ch'an* "production", and *tang* "party". As Chairman of the "Share Production party", Mao Tse-tung has been able to win respect (if not necessarily fondness) for that party by convincing the cynical people of China that production is being properly shared.

WHEN Mao and his men took over mainland China in the closing months of 1949, they were immediately faced with the fundamental problem of patching up a war-eroded economy to make certain that there would be production to share. On top of that gigantic task, the Communists—as self-appointed executors of Sun Yat-sen's call for the re-establishment of a unified, prestigious China—also had to fulfil long-cherished hopes of destroying foreign influence and asserting Chinese power. During their first decade, the Communists set about these tasks with a vigour and degree of success that shook China and the world.

In their first year of rule the Communists were calculatingly rude to Western officials who had stayed on in anticipation of the eventual establishment of diplomatic relations, and they were ruthless in mopping up isolated pockets of Kuomintang supporters. But in the main they were not harsh. To the rank-and-file officials of the Nationalist government and to China's bourgeois industrialists they offered forgiveness and friendly co-operation. They provided appropriate jobs for intellectuals and even tolerated minor political parties.

This domestic mildness was a necessary tactic. In 1949 the Chinese Communist party had fewer than five million members, and the number of Communists experienced in provincial or city government was small. To keep their huge prize running, the new rulers had to rely heavily on all kinds of people—from bus drivers to generals—who had previously served under the Nationalist or the Japanese puppet governments. Mao and his comrades knew they faced a tremendous job. The inflated currency had almost no value. The basic unit, the "Gold Yuan" issued by the Nationalists, had been officially valued at 25 U.S. cents in August 1948, and by the beginning of 1949, it was worth less than a cent. Communications had been virtually destroyed. Bridges had been blown, ships had been sunk and factories throughout the country had fallen idle—in part because many industrialists were taking refuge in British Hong Kong.

Even before South China had fallen to his troops, Mao had declared: "The imperialists count upon our not handling our economic problems well. They stand on the sidelines and await our failure." However, the "mild" policy soon started paying off. Industrialists trickled back from Hong Kong, impressed by the orderly way Communist troops and officials were taking over cities and tempted by Mao's promise that "current policy is to control capitalism, not eliminate it". Mao returned from Moscow in March 1950 with only a niggardly loan of £107 million, but news of this aid heartened planners and workers. By that time inflation was under control, and by October, 90 per cent of the nation's railway lines were back in service.

AS the economy began functioning the honeymoon period of "mild" treatment ended. Violence, terror and suspicion became common. The outside world became aware of this during the Korean War, which started in June 1950. By the end of October, Chinese "volunteers" had engaged American troops along the Yalu River on the Korean-Chinese border, and during the following few months the Chinese forces swept southwards, overwhelming the

Western armies. The Communists had little trouble convincing many Chinese that the United States had intended to invade their country along the Korea-Manchuria route the Japanese had used half a century earlier. With millions of their subjects as roused as Americans would be if a Russian-backed "international force" moved from Cuba through Mexico towards Texas, the Communists skilfully employed the patriotic frenzy to assist them in carrying out tasks on the party list of priorities.

LAND reform was high on that list. In forcing redistribution of land the Communists had three main goals. First, they aimed to pay off a long-standing promise to several hundred million peasants who had either no land at all or not enough land to make a living. Secondly, they hoped that peasants farming for themselves rather than for landlords would produce larger harvests. Thirdly, and possibly most important, they wanted to destroy China's "landlord class", or rural gentry.

Government in rural areas had for long been exercised mainly through the tiny minority of literate men who lived in the country towns and villages. Ideally these men, trained in the Confucian virtues, acted as intermediaries between peasants and government. Enlightened gentry could do much to help conditions in their area, and some did so. Others, less enlightened or themselves caught in the never-ending struggle for survival, perpetuated viciousness. When extra tax levies came, they passed the bulk of the increases on to the poorer peasants. If the peasants could not pay, the gentry would lend them money—at high interest rates. A kindly member of the gentry might finance the education of a bright peasant boy and be honoured by all who knew him; a rogue might seduce a debtor's wife with impunity. But benevolent or brutal, the literati in China's villages tended to share a common trait: they were supporters of the *status quo*. As such, their power had to be broken if the Communists were to be masters of the country.

In 1927, Mao Tse-tung had declared that a revolution was "not the same as inviting people to dinner or writing an essay, or painting a picture or doing fancy needlework . . .". He had insisted that if a revolution was to succeed it would be "necessary to bring about a brief reign of terror in every rural area; otherwise one could never suppress the activities of the counter-revolutionaries in the countryside or overthrow the authority of the gentry".

During the revolutionary land-reform campaign which convulsed large sections of the Chinese countryside from 1950 to 1952, Mao's view that terror was a necessary political tool prevailed. In hundreds of thousands of villages mass trials of "criminals" were held, with peasants acting as both judges and jurors. Peasant justice was meted out with all the fairness to be expected from stirred up lynch mobs anywhere. In some cases peasants driven into a frenzy by Communist agitators beat defendants to death on the spot. Firing-squads, performing before large public audiences, eliminated thousands of members of the "landlord class" from China's countryside. Others died in "reform through labour" camps. Communist-dominated peasant associations took over the gentry's former governing function in the countryside.

THE Communists also used violence and terror to consolidate their power in the cities, flushing out genuine Kuomintang agents and grinding down anyone who questioned party dictates. Millions were charged with being "counter-revolutionaries" and ended up before "people's courts". Often tortured or harassed until they "confessed", these hapless victims of revolutionary justice also furnished practice for the firing-squads and labour for the vast public-works projects. The campaign against counter-revolutionaries also had other uses. When the Communists pushed a "Resist America, Aid Korea" drive for bonds and donations in 1951, awareness of the people's courts undoubtedly helped to loosen purse strings.

Men and women who had responded to the mild policy of the first year by carrying on with their jobs were whipped into line during the notorious "Three-Anti" and "Five-Anti" campaigns. The Three-Anti drive attacked the three evils of corruption, waste, and bureaucratic abuse of power in government, in state industry, and in the expanded party. The targets of the Five-Anti campaign were primarily manufacturers and merchants. The five "evils" were tax evasion, bribery, theft of state assets, utilizing knowledge of state economic projects for private gain, and cheating on labour or materials.

THESE campaigns hit the corrupt and the honest, the innocent and the guilty alike. How much they hurt the régime can never be calculated; many thousands of competent technicians and skilled administrators were killed or dispatched to the labour camps. Moreover, thousands of previously enthusiastic supporters of the régime decided to keep their opinions and knowledge to themselves, or turned into superficially obedient automatons. From the Communists' point of view the drives were valuable in eliminating much genuinely dangerous opposition. They also netted the régime between £350 million and £700 million in confiscated wealth.

In the short run, at least, the Communists' tough policy therefore paid off. By their calculated use of force they got things done, and this earned them respect as masters of an effective government. In Korea, where they heartened Chinese at home and abroad (even the Nationalists in Taiwan) by demonstrating that Chinese troops could defeat Westerners, they did much to generate a feeling of national self-respect—something no government in China had been able to do for a long time.

The terror eventually slackened. After 1953 the Communists moved with considerable caution in domestic affairs. Their ability to push the populace to a point where serious revolt seemed inevitable, and then to avert disaster by backing off to prepare for a later drive, has remained one of the most remarkable phenomena of modern China.

In the countryside, where redistribution of 100 million or more acres to some 300 million peasants resulted in no appreciable increase in government revenues, the party coaxed the peasants towards collectivization. In the growing industrial areas party control over merchants and industrialists increased rapidly. In 1956 almost all firms remaining in the hands of the "national capitalists" were suddenly expropriated and became joint state-private enterprises. As a reward for their "voluntary" co-operation in this move, those capitalists who had not fled or killed themselves during the persuasion period were assigned annual interest payments amounting to about 5 per cent of the value of their former holdings.

The Communists granted this un-Marxian interest payment because they needed the capitalists' know-how. At about the same time they realized too that they would need increased co-operation from non-party intellectuals if they were going to build a powerful modern state in a hurry. The "Hundred Flowers" campaign which they launched to win over the intellectuals succeeded instead, however, in severely jeopardizing the régime.

THE campaign's slogan, "Let a hundred flowers bloom, let a hundred schools of thought contend", was first issued in May 1956. The Communist party officially encouraged criticism of "improper work style" among cadres, but for a year the non-party intellectuals—remembering the terror of the "anti" campaigns—kept their thoughts to themselves. However, constant reassurances by high officials finally set the intellectuals to contending and blooming in the spring of 1957.

Instead of producing bouquets, however, long-muzzled members of the minor political parties, students led by their teachers, and even military men offered up a thorny crop of what party disciplinarians later called "poisonous weeds". The editor-in-chief of a leading non-party paper wrote of the "many critical opinions about the young bonzes"—an allusion to criticism of low-ranking Communists—and pointedly added that "nobody had anything to say about the old bonzes" like Chairman Mao Tse-tung and Premier Chou En-lai. A reporter for the official New China News Agency, himself a Party member for 13 years, openly asserted that China had a "privileged class", and claimed, "all the pork and edible oil have been consumed by the members of the Communist party and cadres". This man even went so far as to "suspect that Chairman Mao . . . committed errors".

THIS storm of criticism quickly spread from Peking to cities all over the country. From Canton came reports of dissatisfaction among peasants and workers. At the Wuhan industrial complex students and faculty members rioted and seized Communist officials. Such unexpected protests against Communist personnel and policy cropped up everywhere.

Alarmed by the growing ferocity and expanding scale of the criticism, Mao clapped the shackles back on the press. Soon came reports of "spontaneous" denunciations of minority political party leaders like Chang Po-chun, Communications Minister, and Lo Lung-chi, Minister of Timber Industry, whose outspoken opinions had attracted widespread attention. The Communists quickly had Chang, Lo and thousands of others "confessing" to a fantastic range of political crimes.

The ensuing "rectification" campaign ruthlessly suppressed dissenting opinion. Chang and Lo were dismissed from office, together with the Minister of Food, who had also spoken too frankly; more than 50 members of the state's National People's Congress were labelled "Rightists" and dismissed from the Congress; hundreds of thousands of officials were also damned as Rightists or sentenced to labour camps. In the only publicized execution, four of the Wuhan school rioters—charged with advocating the return of Chiang Kai-shek—were shot before an audience of 10,000 people. It is unlikely that many more were executed; most of the thousands who paid with their lives for their naïveté in speaking out met their deaths more discreetly and productively. They died as over-worked, underfed prisoners on enormous farm/factory/mining complexes which became an important but unpublished element in Communist China's economy.

The rectification campaign to wipe out the "reactionary" and conservative ideas revealed in the blossoming of the "Hundred Flowers" had a marked influence on Communist party economic policy. Advocates of careful, step-by-step development were swept aside by the campaign's "mighty torrent of Communist ideas", most of which advocated more radical efforts to build the economy. The birth of a policy favouring speedy development by unorthodox means was also hastened by two developments arising out of the relationship between China and the Soviet Union.

FIRST, the Chinese apparently decided that Soviet economic assistance—which amounted to less than £945 million in repayable loans and credits between 1950 and 1957—was on too limited a scale to transform backward, agrarian China quickly into an industrial power. "Capital" for such a transformation would have to come from revolutionary exploitation of China's man—and woman—power.

Second, by the end of 1957 China's leaders had come to believe that the "inevitable" triumph of Communism was at hand. The Russians had agreed to help China to produce nuclear weapons. The Russians had also orbited the world's first space satellite. Obviously they could strike the United States with their long-range missiles. With the Soviet bloc militarily strong, and with the United States in what the Chinese euphorically interpreted as an "ever more serious economic recession", Mao Tse-tung and his supporters felt the time was ripe to push for the realization of Communism at home and abroad.

China is still suffering from the economic and political consequences of Mao's extraordinary miscalculation. The "Great Leap Forward", a myth-creating economic programme which was conceived late in 1957, thrust China night. Production targets for 1958, originally set from about 6 to 20 per cent above 1957 levels, were revised upward again and again. By August 1958 the steel target had been increased from 6.2 million tons to 10.7 million, a 100 per cent rise over 1957. The whole country seemed to be on a gigantic production spree as party propagandists ground out slogans urging steelworkers to surpass Britain's production in 15 years, or proclaiming that one day's achievements in the new China represented 20 years' effort in the old. In all this frenetic activity Mao Tse-tung decided the time had come to establish a revolutionary form of social organization—the people's commune.

The people's commune was supposed to be "the most appropriate organizational form in China for accelerating socialist construction and the transition to Communism". About 65 per cent of China's capital investment in 1958 was budgeted for industry. Agricultural development was to be financed primarily through increased investment of human labour, through reliance on village-made goods and tools, and through decreased food and fuel consumption. The people's communes were designed to provide this "financing" and to combine "economic, cultural, political and military affairs", formerly managed by local governments, "into one entity".

RURAL collectivization was no innovation dreamed up by the Communists. Chinese governments had tried it for centuries, and as late as 1952 the Kuomintang was publishing copies of Chiang Kai-shek's *Chinese Economic Theory*, which advocated "collective farms to save labour and increase production".

In theory Mao's communes seemed a sensible innovation. Everyone was supposed to eat in communal mess halls. Women thus freed from cooking could, and did, swell the work force—a form of capital investment. Communal eating could also save fuel and control the consumption of food. In a poor country like China, where saving one ounce of grain per person per day could pile up more than seven million

into the largest, most spectacular investment of human endeavour the world has ever seen.

Between October 1957 and June 1958 more than 100 million peasants shivered in cold and sweltered in heat, dredging canals and building dykes on massive irrigation projects. From Mukden to Canton, textile factories and blast furnaces operated around the clock; "shock battalions" of field-workers laboured day and tons of food in a year, mess halls made economic sense.

Theoretically, the people's communes were going to change the entire nature of life in China. Children would be raised in public nurseries; a great variety of social services, from haircuts to burials, would be furnished free; almost all property would be owned in common; armies of labourers, operating under the slogan "let politics take command", would perform miracles. Using new farming techniques of close planting and deep ploughing propounded by Chairman Mao, commune members would produce huge surpluses of crops. They would build and run factories, establish schools and erect housing projects—in short, they would create a Communist paradise.

IN the closing months of 1958 Mao's China was leaping towards the Marxist millennium with great bounding strides—or seemed to be. The harvest of food grains in 1957 had supposedly reached 185 million tons; in December 1958 the Communists claimed a fabulous harvest of 375 million tons. Steel production was reported to have more than doubled from 5.3 to 11 million tons, while cotton had leaped from 1.6 to 3.3 million tons. On paper the Great Leap Forward was working out, and the 24,000 communes—encompassing perhaps 500 million peasants—seemed sure of a bright future.

In fact, however, the Great Leap Forward succeeded only on paper—on the reams of paper covered with slogans and grossly inflated statistics. In their haste to produce steel and turn China into a world power, Mao's cadres had bungled badly. With millions of people diverted from agriculture to tending back-yard iron and steel furnaces, planting was neglected and crops were left rotting in the field. Transport was snarled; men and machines were overworked; cropland was damaged by improper ploughing and irrigation; a contradictory flood of orders left peasants sullen and commune cadres frustrated. Even as party propagandists announced ridiculous 1959 targets like 525 million tons of food grains, serious food shortages started plaguing China's cities and countryside.

From the spring of 1959 to the end of 1962 hunger or the fear of hunger was the overriding preoccupation of almost everyone in China. To save face the press continued to stress industrial planning, but China's leaders increasingly turned their attention to agriculture.

In the autumn of 1960 the Chinese Communists realized that they were in a desperate situation. The Russians, angered over Mao Tse-tung's attempt to seize leadership of the world Communist movement, had pulled their advisers out of China and were refusing to consider further aid. The hard-pressed Chinese started buying large quantities of grain from capitalist countries like Canada and Australia.

The winter of 1960-1 was probably Communist China's most trying period to date. Although some people may have starved to death in Kansu province far from the coast, emergency grain stocks and the foreign imports were apparently sufficient to avert mass starvation. But all over the country subsistence rations left millions too weak to resist diseases like influenza and hepatitis. Industrial activity was further reduced, food production given priority.

BY abandoning the communes in everything but name and allowing the peasants to maintain some private plots for growing vegetables or raising pigs or poultry to sell on the open market, the Communists after mid 1962 succeeded in coaxing sufficient food out of the peasantry to get the country back on an adequate diet. As the nation moved into the second half of the 1960s, gradual, rational development of both agriculture and industry seemed likely. But then Mao, for reasons China observers could only guess at, launched his Great Proletarian Cultural Revolution. Primarily a political rather than an economic upheaval, it still showed signs of dislocating the economy almost as badly as had the Great Leap Forward. If that proved true, then all gains would be wiped out and the always grim life would become grimmer still.

CLOUDS OF SMOKE fill the sky above the steelworks of Fushun, Manchuria. Rich in natural resources, Manchuria was seized in 1931 by the Japanese, who expanded its industries. After World War II, it became China's industrial heartland.

A Furious Drive for Modernization

China is pouring immense amounts of human energy into a bitter struggle to increase its industrial capacity and agricultural production. Massive public works have been built, some partly by the manual labour of thousands of workers. To spur food production, the Communists reorganized China's ancient system of family farming, and now peasants work much of the land collectively. Attempting to forcefeed industry, the government came perilously close to dislocating the entire economy, with tragic human consequences. Nevertheless, progress has been made. The basis for light and heavy industry has been laid and essential communications have been expanded. Yet insufficient capital, over-population and the shortage of resources still present serious problems.

GANGS OF WORKERS meticulously sift a scrap-metal dump for usable pieces of steel or iron. Collection of scrap has helped to enlarge China's steel production. Chinese workers often wear gauze masks to help them to avoid colds and influenza.

131

TEENAGE APPRENTICES in a motor-car plant in Nanking learn from a technician (*centre*) who combines teaching with his work. Because of the teacher shortage, every skilled worker must double as an instructor. Special emphasis is placed on obtaining young men and women with a high-school diploma and introducing them to the intricacies of modern manufacturing.

production from the available machinery

WHIRRING SPINDLES in a textile mill in Sian hum at top speed. Six thousand workers live in near-by apartments and dormitories provided at a minimal rent by the government.

FACTORY NEWS is reported on scrolls which hang like laundry on a line. The worker is informed about the achievement of individual work brigades and reminded of party demands.

A WELL-PAID WORKER. a girl runs a machine on the production line of a Manchurian iron and steel mill. Her salary of £14 a month makes her among the highest-paid workers in China.

BOLSTERING MORALE, a political worker hands leaflets to members of a commune—one of the collective units created in 1958 to conduct farming and industry along military lines.

EATING SUPPER, a mobile task-force enjoys a moment's respite near its tents. Forced to move whenever and wherever needed, workers resented disruption of traditional family ties.

UNREALISTIC GOALS of the "Great Leap Forward" led to economic collapse

WORKING A BELLOWS, a peasant on a commune engages in back-yard furnace production of pig iron. The operation of thousands of primitive blast furnaces drained the labour supply, leaving farms short-handed, and resulted in inferior products. Such failures caused the government in 1959 to shift the emphasis from huge communes to smaller production brigades.

campaign to wrest more food from the land

PICKING COTTON, Moslem women work on a farm near an oasis in the Gobi Desert. The Uighurs and other desert nomads have been organized into communes by the Communists.

PLANTING A FIELD, workers operate in teams on a farm commune outside Peking. Many of these communes were established in 1958 as part of a programme called "Great Leap Forward".

HEARING A LECTURE, students from a Peking school cluster around instructors in farming. School children are expected to do manual labour on communes during part of the year.

HUGE DAMS are being built
to produce badly needed electricity
and control the flood-prone rivers

DUSTY CONSTRUCTION WORKERS labour on the San Men dam (*background*), which stretches across the often flooded Yellow River. It is designed to irrigate about six million acres.

PENNANT-BEARING MARCHERS celebrate the completion of the Ming Tombs dam, a massive earth and stone structure built mainly by manual labour of thousands of "volunteer" workers.

*TECHNOLOGY is avidly
promoted by the régime
as it strives for
increases in production*

PROPAGANDA POSTERS proclaim China's
ambitious industrial goals (*background*) at a
1958 exhibition in Peking as two interested
engineers examine the workings of a machine.

GAUNT REFINERY TOWERS are operated by
a swarm of workers at a cracking plant in Yumen, in the north-west province of Kansu where
much of China's oil and gas is concentrated.

MODERN PLANT EQUIPMENT draws an
interested crowd at the 1958 Peking industrial
exhibition. Despite recent setbacks, China still
dreams of becoming a major industrial power.

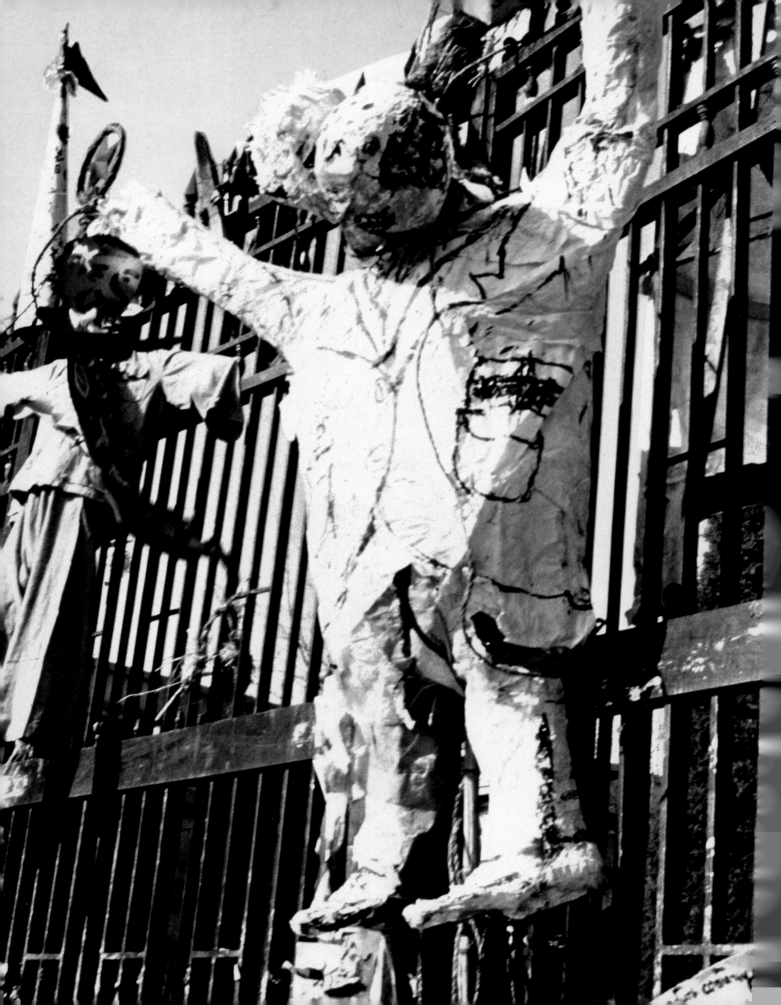

9

The Great Quarrel

FOR public consumption on the 10th anniversary of the People's Republic of China in October 1959, the Secretary-General of the Chinese Communist party, Teng Hsiao-p'ing, piously declared: "The socialist camp headed by the Soviet Union is the reliable guarantee of world peace and human progress." China, Teng continued, "has joined this camp, and shares the same destiny and life-breath . . .".

Less than four years later, Péking's official *Jen Min Jih Pao* (*People's Daily*) presented quite a different view: "Incontrovertible facts show that the Soviet government has sold out the interests of the Soviet people, the interests of the Socialist camp, including [those of] the Chinese people, and the interests of the peace-loving people throughout the world."

An uncritical observer might have thought that China's 1959 acknowledgment of Soviet leadership had reinforced what most people in the outside world had believed all along: that China was a big—but none the less obedient—satellite of the Soviet Union. Serious students of the Chinese scene, however, had never believed that the proud Chinese would play the role of Russian puppets. They thought that the Sino-Soviet alliance would evolve into a form of partnership, possibly one in which each

143

of the two Communist giants would have a separate geographical sphere of influence. Some careful analysts, weighing seemingly innocuous asides, began to claim in the late 1950s that serious differences had arisen between Moscow and Peking. But even these skilled observers were surprised at the violence of the open recrimination which began to reflect the already strained unity of the Communist camp in the summer of 1963.

THE history behind the Russia-China split is long and complicated, but an understanding of how it came about is essential to an understanding of modern China. Moreover, the divergence between the two most powerful Communist nations is of vast importance to the world, for it has already had far-reaching effects upon international events. In the main, the split took place because Russia and China, despite their Marxist bond, are two very different countries with vastly different historical backgrounds and with widely diverging conceptions of how the Communist Utopia may be achieved. For all their advancing years, the men who led China in the 1950s and 1960s were first-generation, idealistic revolutionaries, anxious to get on with the building of a Communist state and a Communist world; the men in charge of Russia in the same period were by and large second-generation revolutionaries, considerably less eager to attempt radical experiments and adventures.

Although the Chinese Communists publicly praised the Russian dictator, Joseph Stalin, while he was alive (and continued to praise him later as a means of defying his successors, they have for long privately held Stalin responsible for policies which nearly destroyed the Chinese Communist party in the 1920s and 1930s. Stalin further dismayed and angered the Chinese at the end of World War II when he demonstrated that he either had no faith in the ability of Mao Tse-tung and his guerrilla armies to take over China, or that he was unwilling to risk trouble in Asia by openly supporting Mao in a fight with the American-backed forces of

Chiang Kai-shek. It is possible, also, that Stalin thought he might gain more for Russia from Chiang than from the intransigent Mao Tse-tung.

First, the U.S.S.R. in 1945 and 1946 removed or destroyed much of Manchuria's heavy industry. This was hardly the action a practised strategist would take if he expected that an ally would ever be able to take over the area—unless he distrusted that ally. Secondly, according to Yugoslav sources, Stalin told the Chinese Communists that since he saw no immediate prospect for their victory over the Nationalists, they should dissolve their armies and join Chiang Kai-shek's government. The Chinese politely agreed—and then proceeded to beat Chiang on their own.

REGARDLESS of what strains Stalin's errors may have placed on the relationship between himself and Mao Tse-tung, one fact is clear: both men realized that mutual co-operation in opposition to Western "imperialism" was in the interests of their respective countries. Under the 1950 Sino-Soviet treaty, Mao received a 5-year, £107 million loan. Although the amount was puny considering China's size and needs, no other aid was available, and the capital, equipment and Soviet technicians supplied to China under the agreement did provide valuable help in early reconstruction. In return the U.S.S.R. obtained useful economic concessions in Sinkiang and Manchuria and China's recognition of Soviet hegemony in the "independent" Mongolian People's Republic.

There was little if any obvious friction between the two countries in the years immediately following Stalin's death in 1953. The first major stresses developed in 1956. That was the year in which the Soviet Premier Nikita Khrushchev began denouncing Stalin and the "cult of personality" that had been built around the dictator during his lifetime. The Chinese comrades, who had a personality cult of their own centring on Chairman Mao, were quietly horrified. They also believed that Khrushchev's extravagantly frank attacks on Stalin—the man for decades acknowledged as the embodiment of Marxist-Leninist wisdom—were extremely harmful to the unity of the world Communist movement. That same year the Chinese acquired more misgivings about Khrushchev's judgment arising out of his inept handling of the revolts in Poland and, particularly, in Hungary.

In the struggle for ideological leadership after 1956, the Chinese and Russians for a time conducted their arguments secretly, preserving the image of Communist solidarity. Neither side criticized the other by name in articles or speeches. All criticism was carried on through diplomatic and party channels, through editorial innuendo and implication, or by attacking straw men.

The Soviets were the first to breach protocol seriously, and Nikita Khrushchev did it in a manner which Mao Tse-tung must have taken as a calculated, personal rebuke. On December 1, 1958, Khrushchev received the then Senator Hubert H. Humphrey of the United States and spent a record 8 hours and 25 minutes with him. In the course of the far-ranging conversation the leader of world Communism remarked, "I have the deepest respect for President Eisenhower, I like President Eisenhower. We want no evil to the United States. . . ." This amicable declaration was fantastically out of tune with Peking's violently anti-American line.

But most disturbing and insulting of all to the Chinese were the Soviet Premier's blasphemies on matters dear to Mao Tse-tung's doctrinal heart. Asked about relations with China, Khrushchev backed off, refusing to comment. Then Humphrey asked for his views on the people's communes—established with great fanfare in China only a few months earlier.

DISREGARDING protocol, Khrushchev gave Humphrey, Mao, and all the rest of the interested world his down-to-earth view on the communes: "They are old-fashioned, they are reactionary. . . . We tried that right after the revolution. It just doesn't work."

Then in a heretical aside which thoroughly justifies Chinese charges that Khrushchev was a "revisionist", the Premier attacked a principle formulated by none other than Karl Marx himself. "You know, Senator, what those communes are based on? They are based on that principle, 'From each according to his abilities, to each according to his needs'. You know that won't work. You can't get production without incentive."

BY the time Krushchev had begun to speak out like this in public, the Chinese Communists had already taken steps to build international support for their own more violent and doctrinaire brand of Communism. As early as 1953 they began to offer economic aid in Asia, and soon had programmes going in Europe, the Middle East, Africa and Latin America. No country with a Communist party was too small or too big to escape their attention.

The extent of China's success in winning support abroad is difficult to assess. One view —over-simplified but partly valid—is that Moscow wins the support of the more developed nations, while Peking wins that of the less developed. The relatively moderate Russian tone, for example, tends to appeal to the Communist parties in Europe; Maoist-style militancy appeals to the Communists in Asian and Latin American countries. But the struggle is complicated by side-issues. China's border fight with India is a case in point.

Demarcation of the border between India and the Tibetan territory now controlled by Communist China involves complex questions left over from British colonial days. But the legal and topographical problems are secondary to political and emotional considerations.

Despite the fact that India for years supported Peking's bid for a United Nations seat, the Chinese for long viewed India's late Prime Minister Jawaharlal Nehru with suspicion. The appeal to the uncommitted Asian and African nations of Nehru's policies of non-alignment with either East or West, and the achievement of social gains by democratic means, constituted a challenge to Mao Tse-tung's call for violent revolution. In addition to that source of friction,

China and India both had historic claims to special interests in Tibet.

In the spring of 1959, anti-Chinese Tibetans in Lhasa launched an open revolt against the Communist rule which had been imposed on Tibet in 1950-1. After weeks of trying to control the situation and suppress all news of the struggle, Peking propagandists suddenly began to claim that "upper-strata reactionaries" had revolted and abducted the Dalai Lama, Tibet's religious head. As a hostage, he had been important to the Chinese in their efforts to control the restless Buddhist region.

THE Chinese clearly expected Nehru to return the Dalai Lama to Tibet if he crossed into India ahead of his Chinese "protectors". Nehru instead granted asylum to the Dalai Lama and large numbers of other Tibetan fugitives. That marked the end of an over-publicized Sino-Indian friendship.

In the autumn of 1959 serious clashes occurred along the borders in Kashmir and the north-east of India. The Soviet press remained carefully neutral, contenting itself with calling the clashes "deplorable". Peking made some displays of negotiating differences but quietly continued patrolling and road building in frontier areas. Late in 1962, after the Indians had infiltrated areas where they had for long ignored the Chinese presence, Mao Tse-tung decided to teach India and other bourgeois-inclined countries a lesson about the necessity of co-operating with Communist China.

Tough troops of the People's Liberation Army launched a brilliant attack. Mao's legions slashed swiftly through poorly trained and equipped Indian army units. Indian weakness was revealed to the whole world. Their mission accomplished, the victorious Chinese wisely halted their advance and offered a peaceful settlement—on their own terms. At the same time, the Chinese Communist press began firing an extremely significant editorial volley at Nehru with side shots at the Soviet Union.

The attack on Nehru was so hostile that reconciliation became virtually impossible. The Peking *People's Daily* made an accusation that the border fighting had been "deliberately provoked" by Nehru. Then, still following the protocol of indirect attack, the paper slanted a blow to include the Soviet Union, asserting that "Indian ruling circles headed by Nehru have become pawns in the international anti-China campaign".

What had the Soviet Union done to deserve this thinly veiled "anti-China" charge? Among other things, Moscow had continued to honour agreements to supply aircraft to the Indians and had publicly expressed "regret" over the border fighting. Peking has since claimed that this mild statement of disapproval "amounted to tipping off the enemy that the Socialist camp was not a solid whole. . . ". But what annoyed the Chinese most was the rapidly accumulating evidence that Khrushchev was pressuring them into abandoning war of any kind as an instrument of policy.

ONE very important thing to remember about Mao Tse-tung and his tactics is that he sees world problems through the eyes of the skilful and successful guerrilla leader he once was. His long fight to win China convinced him of the necessity of violence. One of his principles is: "Political power grows out of the barrel of a gun." Victorious in China, Mao reasons: why not use the gun barrel on the rest of the world? It has long appeared that Mao remains undeterred by the thought of a nuclear holocaust. In 1963 the Russians quoted Mao as declaring at a 1957 Moscow meeting that "if a half of humanity were destroyed [in a nuclear war], the other half would still remain but imperialism would be destroyed entirely and there would be only Socialism in all the world . . .".

Neither Khrushchev nor his successors ever condoned that view. In February 1960, the Warsaw Pact members declared that war would "lead to the death of hundreds of millions of people and the annihilation of whole states . . .". And although the outside world was not to hear of it until more than three years later, Khrushchev had already tried to deprive his belligerent allies of the necessary ingredients for manufacturing their own nuclear weapons.

The angry Chinese version of Khrushchev's action goes as follows: on October 15, 1957, (just 11 days after the launching of the first Sputnik), the Soviets agreed to "supply China with atomic bomb samples and technical materials for the manufacture of atomic bombs". Then in June 1959, the Chinese claim, the Soviets "unilaterally scrapped" the agreement. There now appears to be considerable accuracy in the Chinese story.

ONE month after the signing of the October 1957 agreement, Mao Tse-tung was in Moscow for the 40th anniversary of the Bolshevik revolution. During the celebrations he boasted that ". . . the characteristic of the present situation is that the east wind prevails over the west wind; that is, the strength of Socialism exceeds the strength of imperialism". Anticipating the forging of a Chinese nuclear shield and increased Soviet support for his militant views, Mao had reason to appear confident.

But somewhere along the line Khrushchev must have had second thoughts. Precisely when is unclear. Late in July 1958 the Soviet Premier and his Defence Minister made a secret visit to China. On August 8, after the visitors' departure, came the announcement of a Soviet agreement to help China to build 47 major industrial projects. Then on August 23 the Communists launched a massive artillery attack on Quemoy. That attack brought the U.S.A. to the brink of war in the Taiwan Strait. Did Khruschev initiate, oppose, or simply give tacit consent to that bombardment—or did he even know it was in the works? No one outside the Communist world knows the answer, but there are indications of Khrushchev's thinking.

According to the record, Khrushchev wrote two letters to President Eisenhower in September, blaming the U.S.A. and Nationalist China for the trouble. To this extent he did back his allies. But Khrushchev also stressed "peaceful coexistence of all states . . ." and claimed that Russia was "in favour of not allowing the beginning of military conflicts . . .".

This bit of correspondence may have been an example of Communist duplicity. However, considering that in eight weeks of intermittent air skirmishes over the Taiwan Strait the American-supplied Nationalist Air Force lost only 6 planes and shot down 36 M.I.G.s, blasting some of them with air-to-air "Sidewinder" missiles, it seems strange that the Soviets never provided their allies with the Russian version of this weapon. Perhaps Premier Khrushchev, soon to be telling Senator Humphrey his doubts about the economic soundness of the Chinese communes, was already doubtful about Peking's charges of Nationalist and American military provocation.

Still, as late as February 1959 Khrushchev must have thought he could use economic pressure to keep Mao Tse-tung in line. On February 7 the Soviet Premier signed an agreement increasing—from 47 to 78—the number of industrial projects which he had agreed to help to build the previous August. This gesture of fraternity envisaged an eight-year period during which Soviet technicians would assist China in building metallurgical, chemical, oil-refining and electric power plants. Worth nearly £4.5 million, they were to be paid for by Chinese exports to the Soviet Union.

THIS agreement was signed almost immediately after the finish of the Soviet Communist party's 21st Congress, in which Khrushchev had put great emphasis on the peaceful nature of the Soviet Seven-Year Plan. Even then Khrushchev was claiming that his thesis that "war is not fatally inevitable" had been justified. He was also stressing the desirability of a "joint stand for the banning of nuclear weapons and nuclear tests" and the establishment of "a zone free of atomic weapons" in the Far East.

In his speech to the Soviet Congress, China's delegate—Premier Chou En-lai—had ignored any reference to nuclear-free zones. He spoke instead of "eternal and unbreakable" Sino-Soviet friendship, and he read a message from

The Great Quarrel

Chairman Mao praising Chairman Khrushchev's "correct leadership". On the surface at least Khrushchev's promise of economic assistance was getting results; the Chinese were paying for that aid with politeness.

As the spring and summer of 1959 passed into autumn, however, the Chinese had an increasingly difficult time maintaining a façade of politeness in their public relations with their supposed benefactor. The scrapping of the atomic weapons agreement in June was just one of many Chinese frustrations that year. Economically China was in terrible difficulties. Everyone—including the Russians—knew that the 1958 Great Leap Forward claims of achievement and the target set for 1959 were ludicrous.

Politically China was also in very bad shape. "Some comrades"—a phrase frequently used by party dialecticians to attack members deviating from the party line—had opposed the Great Leap Forward and the people's communes. Some, including the Defence Minister, Marshal P'eng Teh-hauai, may have sought support for their views from the Russians. Even as the announcement of P'eng's removal from office was being prepared, Khrushchev was flying to the capitalist United States for two weeks of politicking with the "enemy". The day he reached Washington, Peking's *People's Daily* warned of the danger of peace offensives, and reminded all good Communists of Mao Tse-tung's dictum that imperialism's "fundamental nature cannot be changed. Till their doom the imperialist elements will never lay down the butcher-knife, nor will they ever become Buddhas."

THE old Communist Khrushchev knew for whom the *People's Daily* reminder was intended. After two weeks in the United States and an overnight stop in Moscow, he flew on to Peking for the celebration of the régime's 10th anniversary. Before 5,000 banquet guests, including representatives from 87 countries, the Soviet Premier delivered some frank remarks.

Khrushchev reported his impression that President Eisenhower understood "the need to relax international tensions". All Communists, he declared, "must do everything possible to preclude war as a means of settling outstanding questions". Then after speaking of the strength of the Communist camp, he warned that ". . . this certainly does not mean we should test the stability of the capitalist system by force . . . the people would never support those who took it into their heads to act in this way".

AND that, for all practical purposes, was the beginning of the end of the Sino-Soviet alliance. No communiqué was issued when Khrushchev left Peking, but his farewell remarks at the airport indicated that private talks with Mao could hardly have been cordial. Without mentioning China, he declared that "we Communists of the Soviet Union" felt a sacred duty to "liquidate the cold war".

When the Soviet Union, Great Britain and the United States signed a limited nuclear test-ban agreement in Moscow in the summer of 1963, the Communists of the Soviet Union could claim that at least a step had been taken towards liquidating the East-West Cold War. But Khrushchev's Communists had involved themselves, perhaps inextricably, in a new Cold War. Peking called the test-ban treaty "rotten to the core", and declared, "China of, course, cannot be a party to it". In return, Moscow stated that China's leaders could never "wash off the shame" of gambling "on the death of hundreds of millions of people, including Chinese, in thermonuclear war".

After Khrushchev's eclipse, China's nuclear tests, and U.S. escalation of the war in Vietnam, some Moscow-Peking rapprochement seemed possible. But none came. When First Secretary Leonid Brezhnev invited China to the 23rd Soviet party Congress in March 1966, Peking refused, charging the Soviets with scheming with the United States "to sell out the struggle of the Vietnamese people" and to "build a ring" around China. The Red Guards have reviled the Soviet Union and its "revisionism" in the strongest possible terms.

The once vaunted alliance had deteriorated into a nagging, disruptive quarrel.

A mob of young Hong Kong Chinese hurls stones at helmeted police during the riots that rocked the British crown colony in mid 1967.

Prosperous, Sensitive Outposts Along the Border

On the edge of Communist China lie British Hong Kong and Nationalist Taiwan. Both pose a problem for the mainland's government, Taiwan because of its booming economy, aided by the U.S.A., and Hong Kong because it is a flourishing outpost of the hated "Colonialists" perched at China's back door. Were it not for the presence of the U.S. Seventh Fleet, Communist China might long since have overwhelmed Taiwan. Hong Kong might have been annexed, too, but for its role as a vital market place for Chinese exports. However, anti-British riots there in 1967 seemed to indicate that worse trouble might be brewing.

149

DESPERATE REFUGEES *once streamed into British territory although in recent*

NEAR THE BORDER, British government troops round up refugees who have nearly succeeded in crossing the mountains into Hong Kong. All along the crown colony's land and sea frontier the British keep up constant patrols for detecting illegal immigration. Because Hong Kong's police are vigilant, many refugees have undertaken the hazardous journey to no avail.

years the flow has been reduced to a trickle

AT THE BARRACKS set up for refugees a young man registers. Although Communist guards frequently shoot at escapees, during 1962 they inexplicably let thousands cross unopposed.

OUTSIDE THE COMPOUND a crowd of Hong Kong residents gathers to look for familiar faces among the refugees. Only 50 immigrants a day are legally admitted into Hong Kong.

ON THE WAY BACK to the Communist border (*right*), refugees lean from a bus to receive parcels of food and clothing. The British sent refugees back during the 1962 immigration flood.

FESTOONED LAUNDRY testifies to crowded conditions in the housing blocks built for low-income families. Despite its many refugees, Hong Kong has avoided mass unemployment.

A RESETTLEMENT PROJECT lies on the mainland area of Kowloon (*foreground*). The harbour, once a port for opium-runners, lies between Kowloon and Hong Kong island (*background*).

CROWDED HONG KONG, *a British colony since 1842, surges with activity as one of Asia's busiest commercial centres*

A CONGESTED STREET on Hong Kong island in the old business district of the city is jammed with cars and trams. More than 99 per cent of the population of four million is Chinese.

farming area in South-East Asia

PATTERNS OF COUNTRYSIDE reflect the meticulous use of land. Only by generous application of chemical fertilizer is it possible to feed 13 million people on the limited acreage.

FIELDS OF RICE are worked by a farmer who carefully replaces damaged seedlings. The Nationalists' land reform has enabled 86 per cent of all farmers to own all or part of their fields.

TRAYS OF TAPIOCA, a substance used in fabric finishing, are prepared by workers and set out to dry in the sun. Farm employees earn cash income from such secondary occupations.

WELL-DRESSED CHILDREN play in an attractively decorated nursery that is operated by a farmers' association in order to free adults for work in the fields. Besides such nurseries and a

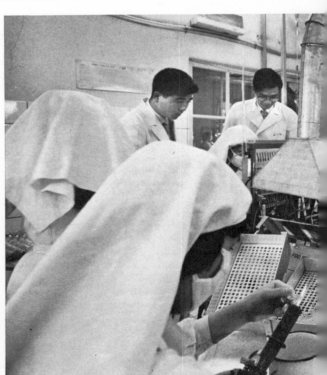

Masked technicians inspect test-tubes containing drugs. Wide use of

SHIPBUILDING at Keelung, a port on the north side of the island, proceeds as workmen assemble mammoth bulkheads. U.S. aid has encouraged commerce and foreign investment.

complete system of primary and intermediate schools, Taiwan has 78 institutions of higher learning. Many university students from Taiwan seek advanced study and careers abroad.

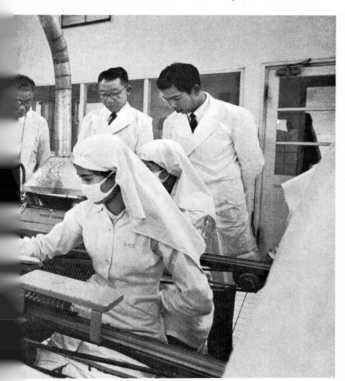

antibiotics has contributed to the success of rural health programmes.

A PRODUCTION LINE turns out diesel-driven power tillers, which are also used to haul produce to market. Other industries specialize in aluminium, plastics and electrical appliances.

PROSPERITY gives Taiwan a standard of living that is one of the highest in Asia

BASTIONS on guard against the Communists, the Nationalist islands are defended by men who await their orders to counter-attack

CONCEALED TUNNELS dot the island of Quemoy, a Gibraltar-like stronghold not far from Communist positions. Honeycombed with fortifications, Quemoy has withstood repeated Communist shelling.

AGEING LEADERS of the Republic of China, Generalissimo and Madame Chiang Kai-shek (*opposite*) sit in a drawing-room of their suburban Taipei home. Chiang has often vowed to return to the mainland.

SKILLED JET PILOTS, who are highly respected by U.S. advisers, meet for flight instructions. The outnumbered Nationalist Air Force scored stunning victories over Communist M.I.G.s in 1958 battles.

YOUNG RED GUARDS in a truck proudly
hold a red banner and a picture of Mao
Tse-tung as they parade through Canton
in early 1967. Mao closed China's schools,
thus releasing hordes of young people to
demonstrate for his Cultural Revolution.

10

Invalid among Nations

SOME of the most worrying questions in
the world hinge on what is going on in
China today and what that country may do
beyond its borders tomorrow.

All around the periphery of this huge land
—in the Soviet Union, Mongolia, Korea, Japan, Taiwan, Hong Kong, South-East Asia, India, Pakistan and Afghanistan—what China
does or may do will affect all sorts of people,
from political strategists to conscription-age
youths. To people far from Asia—to farmers in
Australia and Canada, to taxpayers in America,
to European businessmen, to impatient revolutionaries in Latin America and Africa—what

happens in the world's most populous country
during the next few years and next few decades
can be of vast importance.

With the exception of the Soviet Union, Peking's neighbours are all smaller or weaker than
China. Rich resources of oil, rice and rubber in
South-East Asia—or the necessity of creating a
wartime diversion from overwhelming internal
problems—might tempt a desperate Communist régime to move against one or more Asian
neighbours. In Vietnam, where Chinese influence has waxed and waned for centuries, China
and the U.S.A. are in dangerous confrontation.
China also supports "liberation movements"

in Laos, Thailand and Malaysia; the U.S.A. counters with military and economic aid. Everywhere, overseas Chinese are suspect.

China in the 1960s has been ruled by proud, ageing men devoted to canonizing the "thought of Mao Tse-tung" and sowing world revolution. If these men felt that the nation's security or ideological honour was at stake, they had the power to involve China's obedient millions in a war that could expand into world-wide nuclear conflict.

THE fact was that China, calling limited test-ban agreements a "fraud", had become a nuclear threat. Chinese scientists, some trained in the U.S.A. and in Russia, had produced and tested enough nuclear devices to give China atomic warheads deliverable by aircraft, with production of some ballistic missile "nukes" possible before 1970. While this armoury was puny compared to American or Russian weaponry, it was a danger to peace.

But the basic factor which had caused China to become a very troubled country in recent centuries, and which would keep it a potentially troublesome nation in the future, was its already huge and still-growing population. China today has more than 700 million people and roughly 15 million additional people must be fed and clothed each year from a severely limited amount of arable land. This is an enormous, aggravating burden for any government. Despite all the publicity devoted to industrial development, China remains a predominantly agricultural country. And consider what has happened recently in the most essential sphere of agriculture: food grain production.

According to the best available estimates, the 1958 harvest of 193 million tons was the largest Communist China ever had. Despite careless harvesting, people in most parts of the country had enough to eat. Then three bad harvests hit China hard. The harvest slumped from 193 million tons in 1958 to 168 million tons in 1959. The harvest of 1960 was even worse, producing only 162 million tons, and the 1961 yield of 167 million tons was only slightly

better. These failures dangerously reduced reserve stocks, virtually eliminated exports, and brought severe food shortages to many areas.

The Chinese Communists met the crisis with drastic measures. They tightened rationing and reduced spending on cherished industrial projects. They bought large quantities of wheat from three non-Communist countries—Australia, Canada and France. These measures prevented what propagandists on Taiwan have long been prophesying — large-scale risings by hunger-maddened peasants and rebellious army units. Their rations assured, Mao Tse-tung's troops remained loyal and the peasants apathetic. Then, responding to mild profit incentives, China's resilient peasants brought agriculture out of the terrible slump. Total food grain production for 1963 was probably very close to the reasonably good 1962 figure of 180 million tons. The immediate threat of starvation was averted. But what about the future?

The long-range outlook was bleak. Starting in 1961 China began importing about five million tons of grain and flour a year. This meant an average annual expenditure of more than £90 million—money that could otherwise have gone to bolster China's still inadequate industrial capacity. And while these imports were bridging the gap between what China consumed and what its peasants produced, that costly gap was widening: China had perhaps 660 million people to feed with the 193-million-ton bumper harvest of 1958; the 180-million-ton harvest of 1964 plus 5 million imported tons had to be stretched for more than 700 million persons. In brief, there was approximately 10 per cent less grain *per capita* in 1964 than in 1958.

AN obvious solution to this problem would have been to plant more crops and carry out a mass birth-control programme. These two procedures were more easily recommended than carried out. Arable land was being farmed at or near maximum capacity; to obtain increased acreage from land reclamation schemes would require huge outlays of money and labour, and peasants, valuing sons as one sure means of achieving security in old age, were not likely soon to change their ways.

THE Chinese Communists implied that much of their difficulty stemmed from the Soviet Union's unfriendly acts and niggardly aid policy. And they had a point. Although the Soviets had provided £150 million in cash loans between 1950 and 1954, they had not supplied the Chinese with any outright grants. And all the approximately £1,000 million provided in low-interest loans and credits had been earmarked for specific projects, affording the Chinese little flexibility.

But what if the Russian Communists had been willing and able to finance the transformation of China from a subsistence-level agricultural society to an industrialized nation with a well-developed supporting agriculture? How much money would have been needed?

One way to look at this question is to consider an area where something of this sort has been done. That area is Taiwan, the seat of Chiang Kai-shek's Nationalist government. Here, after the ignominious retreat of 1949, a determined group of talented men has begun to build a new economy, increasing over-all agricultural productivity by more than 93 per cent, expanding light industry and adding urban facilities for a growing populace.

Visitors to Taiwan, having heard stories of the chaos and corruption of the régime's final years on the mainland, come away amazed. The island's cities and villages are full of active, well-fed, adequately clothed people. In the flatlands and hills grow fine crops of rice, sugar cane, tea, oranges and pineapples.

On this island, where resident Taiwanese were the major landowners, the government carried out a highly successful land reform. This reform, combined with the expansion of the primary school system established by the Japanese, has made Taiwan's peasants among the most prosperous and literate in Asia. The Kuomintang, pointing to the fact that Taiwan is in a state of war with the mainland, has prevented the formation of a genuine political op-

position. However, the climate of economic well-being and an effective security system have helped to dissipate political discontent. By and large, Taiwan presents the picture of a well-run country with seemingly good future prospects.

Since the Nationalists have apparently been successful on Taiwan, why should not they or some other government be able to repeat the performance on the mainland? In the answer to this question also lies the key to the earlier question about the amount of money necessary for mainland China's development.

An indispensable element in Taiwan's good showing to date has been the more than £530 million of economic aid which the United States gave to the Nationalist government between 1950 and 1965. This figure does not include the more than £890 million charged in the same period to military aid, but channelled in part to the civilian economy. Thus the United States was supporting the Nationalist government with an economic subsidy averaging just under £35 million a year. From 1950 to 1965, Taiwan's population increased from about 7.6 million to almost 13 million. Estimating roughly, the United States contributed £3 10s. a year between 1949 and 1965 for the economic well-being of every person on Taiwan.

SOME observers have suggested that an equivalent amount of outside aid *per capita* would bring comparable well-being to the mainland—even though it has a population roughly 60 times that of Taiwan. The idea is unrealistic. Not only would the required amount be astronomical—some £2,500 million a year—and clearly beyond the means of any outside helper or helpers, but the economic situations in the two places cannot be compared. The available resources and levels of consumption on Taiwan and the mainland are not the same. Moreover, there would be little possibility of exercising the kind of managerial control and supervision on the mainland—regardless of the régime in power—which has been possible on Taiwan.

None the less, there is no escaping the fact that regardless of what kind of government is in power the magnitude of the mainland problem is tens of times greater than the one that existed on Taiwan in the early 1950s. There is no ready solution to the dreary problem of more than 700 million people living on too little land, with too little capital to increase the productivity of that land. The resulting frustrations constitute a chronic threat to international peace. And when this threat is backed by revolutionary zeal, it becomes a problem for the entire world.

FURTHER complicating the situation is the matter of the Nationalist régime and its impatience with the United State's unwillingness to support a counter-attack against the mainland. The situation on Taiwan is a peculiar one. The President of the Republic of China is recognized by the United States as the ruler of all China, and by treaty he is to be defended by the U.S.A. against Communist attack. However, the United States and Nationalist China have also agreed that the Chinese forces may not undertake a military offensive against the mainland without prior American agreement.

Chiang Kai-shek, together with his elder son Chiang Ching-kuo and Madame Chiang, however, have continued to insist that it was necessary to hit China with large-scale commando raids and even preventive strikes against Communist nuclear sites. They have argued that such attacks would touch off anti-Communist risings and defections, forestall the Communists from launching nuclear attacks and thwart Peking's aims in Vietnam. While few Americans shared these views, there was always the possibility that frustrated Nationalists might launch an all-or-nothing assault by themselves.

Potentially still more serious is the unrest and disorder visible on the mainland of China since Mao Tse-tung launched his Great Proletarian Cultural Revolution in the last days of 1965. The most publicized evidence of this disorder was the activities of the Red Guards—the gangs of students released from the schools Mao had closed who roamed the countryside and the cities, burning books, humiliating and even torturing intellectuals, whom they accused of

"bourgeois tendencies", invading factories, where they chanted Maoist slogans at the workers, and fomenting riots in which, if reports seeping out of the mainland are correct, hundreds and perhaps thousands of people were killed.

But more important than the activities of the Red Guards, in the view of many experts, were other, more profound, signs of trouble. Several of China's provinces appeared to be in revolt against the Cultural Revolution, and in one of the nation's most important cities, Wuhan, the local military commander openly defied Mao. And there were shifts at the top. Liu Shao-ch'i, the government's Chairman, was savagely denounced—this being all the more significant because Liu had been considered Mao's heir apparent. The question arose as to who would, or could, rule China in the event of Mao's death, with some observers predicting that the country, unified with so much difficulty, might again break up into groups of provinces, each section ruled by a strongman. Mao's behaviour made it evident that Defence Minister Lin Piao was his choice as successor, but Lin seemed to be in frail health. Indeed, all the potential leaders, such as Chou En-lai, were ageing and no younger men capable of taking power had made their appearance. Thus even greater chaos and lack of direction seemed to loom should Mao, who initiated the disorders of the Cultural Revolution, suddenly pass from the scene.

WHATEVER happened, the central dilemma of what to do about the gigantic mainland nation with its overwhelming population and its recurrent food shortage would remain. Until that problem could be solved—and perhaps only miracles of agricultural technology, nuclear development or synthetic food production could achieve a solution—China would remain what it had been for a century: a dangerous invalid among nations, a second-class power unable to organize itself for greatness in the modern world, a land of hard-working, suffering people who could only wonder when a day of magnificence worthy of their heritage would arrive.

A lone figure gazes out from the portico of the Buddhist shrine at Yun-Kang, built in the fifth century A.D. near the Gobi Desert.

A STOIC PATIENCE, which has helped the Chinese to endure hardships . . .

A woman worker of the Wuhan iron works pauses to remove her mask.

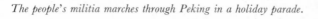

The people's militia marches through Peking in a holiday parade.

...in the past, will be needed more than ever as they enter into new periods of

travail and change in their painful search for an elusive power and prosperity

Appendix

HISTORICAL DATES

B.C.

*c.*360,000 Men of a primitive species called *Sinanthropus pekinensis* establish themselves in the lower Yellow River valley

*c.*2200-1700 Era of the legendary Hsia Dynasty

*c.*1700-1100 The Shang Dynasty flourishes in the Yellow River valley

*c.*1100-800 Kings of the Chou Dynasty consolidate and extend the central power to the Yangtze valley

771-256 Chou hegemony dwindles as warring states manoeuvre for power

221-206 The Ch'in Dynasty is founded by Cheng, the "First Emperor", who unites China. His successor is murdered after a three-year reign

202-195 Liu Pang, king of a neighbouring state, founds the Han Dynasty

140-87 The Emperor Wu Ti extends Chinese power into western Asia, Korea and South-East Asia

A.D.

9-23 Wang Mang, a nephew of the Empress Dowager, usurps the throne and attempts to redistribute land to the peasants

25-220 The Han Dynasty is restored. Its forces conquer Vietnam and move into Sinkiang, exacting tribute from kingdoms as far west as Afghanistan. Buddhism enters China through Central Asia

220-589 After the collapse of the Han, the country is divided into warring kingdoms. The period is known as that of the "three kingdoms and six dynasties"

590-618 Sui emperors again consolidate China, rebuild the Great Wall and employ five million people in construction of an elaborate water transport system

618 Li Yuan and his son found the T'ang Dynasty

960 After a period of disunity, the Sung Dynasty is founded

1271-1292 Marco Polo makes his historic journey to China and South-East Asia

1279 The Mongol Yuan Dynasty completes the conquest of China

1356-1382 The Mongols are driven out of China. The Ming Dynasty is founded

1405-1433 Ming emperors send huge sea expeditions as far as Africa

1514-1600 Western traders attempt to establish trade relations

1582-1610 Father Matteo Ricci, a Jesuit, establishes the first Roman Catholic mission in China

1644-1662 The Manchus conquer the country and establish a new dynasty

1793 Lord Macartney tries unsuccessfully to establish British trade relations with China

1796-1835 Emperor Chia Ch'ing prohibits importation of opium, but the traffic increases to some 19,000 chests annually

1839 Commissioner Lin Tse-hsu is assigned to Canton and forces foreigners to surrender £4 million worth of opium. The Opium War between China and the Western powers begins

1842 The Opium War is settled by the Treaty of Nanking. Five ports are opened for trading; Hong Kong is ceded to Britain; and the Western powers receive legal jurisdiction over their own nationals in China

1853-1864 The T'ai P'ing rebels capture Nanking and hold it as their capital

1858 Foreign nations force the signing of the Treaty of Tientsin, by which China grants still further concessions

1894-1895 Sino-Japanese War culminates in the Treaty of Shimonoseki, under which extensive concessions are granted to Japan

1895 Sun Yat-sen leads an abortive revolt against the Manchus

1898 Emperor Kuang Hsu tries unsuccessfully to modernize China during "100 Days" of reform

1898-1900 Rebellions become widespread. Anti-foreign and anti-Christian agitation increases

1900-1901 Foreign legations in Peking are seized during the Boxer Rising. In retaliation, foreign nations force the Chinese to pay immense indemnities

1911-1912 Successful revolution brings the overthrow of the Manchu Dynasty. Sun Yat-sen is chosen as first President of the Republic of China but is forced out by politicians from the North

1913 Sun Yat-sen launches another revolt in an effort to bring unity to the country. It fails, and he flees to Japan

1921 The Chinese Communist party is organized at meetings held in and near Shanghai

1924 After promises of Russian aid to Sun's party, the Kuomintang, allows Communists to become members. Chiang Kai-shek is made head of the Kuomintang's new Whampoa Military Academy

1925 Sun Yat-sen dies

1926-1928 Chiang Kai-shek launches an expedition against the northern war lords and eventually breaks their power

1927 Chiang crushes the Communists in Shanghai. Mao Tse-tung stages an unsuccessful rising, then retires to Chingkangshan, where he draws supporters

1934-1935 After attacks by the Nationalists, Mao leads his followers northwards on the Long March

1937 Japan invades China. Nationalists and Communists form a united front to fight the Japanese

1945-1947 At U.S. urging, Mao and Chiang confer on the formation of a coalition government

1949 The Communists capture Peking. On October 1, Mao establishes the People's Republic of China. Nationalist government flees to Taiwan

1947-1952 The Communists begin land reform. Opponents—or suspected opponents—of the régime are executed or sent to labour camps

1950 The Korean War begins. Chinese "volunteers" cross the Yalu to fight U.N. troops

1953 The Korean War ends

1955 Mao Tse-tung orders collectivization of farms

1956-1957 During the "Hundred Flowers" campaign the régime receives six weeks of criticism. The critics are punished

1958 Mao initiates the Great Leap Forward programme and reorganizes the country into communes. Industrial output rises, but the gains are exaggerated

1959 Tibetan rising brings harsh reprisals from Peking

1959 Mao Tse-tung relinquishes the chairmanship of the government to Liu Shao-ch'i but remains head of the Communist party. The Communists gradually de-emphasize the commune grogramme

1962 Conflict over territory in Ladakh and north-eastern India precipitates border warfare between India and China

1963 Dispute between China and the Soviet Union over the appropriate road to achieve Communism breaks into the open

1965 Great Proletarian Cultural Revolution begins

1967 China explodes its first hydrogen bomb

FOR FURTHER READING

CHAPTER 1: AN IMMENSE, CROWDED LAND

Buck, John L., *Land Utilization in China.* University of Chicago Press, 1937.

Cressy, George B., *China's Geographic Foundations.* McGraw-Hill, 1934. *Land of the 500 Million.* McGraw-Hill, 1956.

Ho, Ping-ti, *Studies on the Population of China.* Harvard University Press, 1959.

Hsu, Francis L. K., *Americans and Chinese.* Cresset Press, 1955.

Hu, Chang-tu, *China, Its People, Its Society, Its Culture.* Mayflower, 1961.

Lang, Olga, *Chinese Family and Society.* Yale University Press, 1946.

Murphey, Rhoades, *Shanghai, Key to Modern China.* Harvard University Press, 1953.

Shen, Tsung-han, *Agricultural Resources of China.* Cornell University Press, 1951.

Yang, C. K., *The Chinese Family in the Communist Revolution.* Technology Press, Cambridge, Mass., 1959. *A Chinese Village in Early Communist Transition.* Technology Press, Cambridge, Mass., 1959.

Yang, Martin, *A Chinese Village.* Kegan Paul, Trench Trubner, 1947.

CHAPTER 2: DYNASTIES OF LEGEND AND POWER

Creel, Herrlee Glessner, *The Birth of China.* Peter Owen, 1958.

Goodrich, L. Carrington, *A Short History of the Chinese People.* (2nd ed.) Allen & Unwin, 1957.

Latourette, Kenneth Scott, *The Chinese. Their History and Culture.* Macmillan, 1946.

Li Chi, *The Beginnings of Chinese Civilization.* 2 vols. University of Washington Press, 1934.

Reischauer, Edwin O., and Fairbank, John K., *East Asia: The Great Tradition.* Allen & Unwin, 1961.

Watson, Burton, *Records of the Grand Historian of China, translated from the Shih Chi of Ssu-ma Ch'ien.* 2 vols. Columbia University Press, 1961.

CHAPTER 3: FOREIGN CONTACTS

Cranmer-Byng, J. L., ed., *An Embassy to China.* Longmans, Green, 1962.

Dunne, George H., *Generation of Giants.* Burnes & Oates, 1962.

Gallagher, Louis J., *China in the Sixteenth Century: The Journals of Matthew Ricci, 1583-1610.* (Translation.) Random House, New York, 1953.

Hart, Henry H., *Venetian Adventurer.* (Rev. ed.) Stanford University Press, 1947.

Reischauer, Edwin O., *Ennin's Travels in T'ang China.* Ronald Press, New York, 1955.

Vernadsky, George, *The Mongols and Russia.* Yale University Press, 1953.

CHAPTER 4: THE ARTS

Boyd, Andrew, *Chinese Architecture and Town Planning. 1500 B.C.-A.D. 1911.* Alec Tiranti, 1962.

Cahill, James, *Chinese Painting,* Skira, Geneva, 1960.

Chiang Yee, *Chinese Calligraphy.* Harvard University Press, 1954.

Hightower, James R., *Topics in Chinese Literature.* Harvard University Press, 1962.

Hsia, C. T., *A History of Modern Chinese Fiction.* Yale University Press, 1961.

Hsu, Kai-yu, *Twentieth Century Chinese Poetry.* Doubleday, New York, 1963.

Hung, William, *Tu Fu, China's Greatest Poet.* Harvard University Press, 1952.

Mote, Frederick W., *The Poet Kao Ch'i.* Princeton University Press, 1962.

Sickman, Laurence, and Soper, Alexander, *The Art and Architecture of China.* Penguin Books, 1956.

Waley, Arthur, *The Life and Times of Po Chu-i.* Allen & Unwin, 1949. *The Poetry and Career of Li Po.* Allen & Unwin, 1951. *Yuan Mei: Eighteenth Century Chinese Poet.* Allen & Unwin, 1957. Trans. of *The Book of Songs.* Allen & Unwin, 1937.

Wu Ch'eng-en, *Monkey.* Trans. by Arthur Waley. Allen & Unwin, 1942.

Willett, William, *Chinese Art.* Penguin Books, 1958.

CHAPTER 5: RELIGION AND PHILOSOPHY

Burke, James Cobb, *My Father in China.* Farrar & Rinehart, New York, 1942.

Chan, Wing-tsit, *Religious Trends in Modern China.* Columbia University Press, 1953.

Creel, H. G., *Chinese Thought from Confucius to Mao Tse-tung.* Mentor Books, New York, 1960. *Confucius and the Chinese Way.* Harper & Brothers, New York, 1960.

Delza, Sylvia, *Body and Mind in Harmony: T'ai Chi Ch'uan.* David McKay, New York, 1961.

Fung, Yu-lan, *A History of Chinese Philosophy.* Trans. by Derk Bodde. Henri Vetch, Peiping: Allen & Unwin, 1937.

Latourette, Kenneth Scott, *A History of Christian Missions in China.* S.P.C.K., 1929.

Waley, Arthur, *Three Ways of Thought in Ancient China.* Allen & Unwin, 1939. *The Way and Its Power.* Allen & Unwin, 1934.

Welch, Holmes, *The Parting of the Way.* Methuen, 1958.

Werner, E. T. C., *A Dictionary of Chinese Mythology.* Julian Press, New York, 1961.

Yang, C. K., *Religion in Chinese Society.* University of California Press, 1961.

CHAPTER 6: CENTURY OF HUMILIATION

Chiang Kai-shek, *China's Destiny* (an authorized translation of the original work), Macmillan, New York, 1947; (unauthorized translation of the original work, with notes by Philip Jaffe), Dennis Dobson, 1947. *Soviet Russia in China.* Harrap, 1957.

Dennett, Tyler, *Americans in Eastern Asia.* Barnes & Noble, 1941.

Fleming, Peter, *The Siege at Peking.* Rupert Hart-Davis, 1959.

Hsu, Leonard S., *Sun Yat-sen, His Political and Social Ideals.* University of Southern California Press, 1933.

Latourette, Kenneth Scott, *A History of Modern China.* Penguin Books, 1954.

Morse, Hosea Ballou, *The International Relations of the Chinese Empire.* 3 vols. Longmans, Green, 1910-18.

Sharman, Lyon, *Sun Yat-sen, His Life and Its Meaning. A Critical Biography.* John Day, New York, 1934.

Swisher, Earl, *China's Management of the American Barbarians.* Far Eastern Publications, Yale University, 1953.

Tan, Chester C., *The Boxer Catastrophe.* Columbia University Press, 1955.

T'ang Leang-li, *The Inner History of the Chinese Revolution.* George Routledge & Sons, 1930.

Teng Ssu-yu, and Fairbank, John K., *China's Response to the West.* Harvard University Press, 1961.

Tong, Hollington K., *Chiang Kai-shek, Soldier and Statesman.* Hurst & Blackett, 1938.

Vinacke, Harold M., *A History of the Far East in Modern Times.* (6th ed.) Allen & Unwin, 1960.

Waley, Arthur, *The Opium War Through Chinese Eyes.* Allen & Unwin, 1958.

CHAPTER 7: RISE OF THE COMMUNISTS

Brandt, Conrad, *Stalin's Failure in China, 1924-1927.* Harvard University Press, 1958.

Compton, Boyd, *Mao's China: Party Reform Documents, 1942-1944.* University of Washington Press, 1952.

Feis, Herbert, *The China Tangle.* Princeton University Press, 1953.

Isaacs, Harold, *The Tragedy of the Chinese Revolution.* (2nd ed.) Stanford University Press, 1961.

Lewis, John Wilson, *Leadership in Communist China.* Cornell University Press, 1963.

Mao Tse-tung, *Selected Military Writings.* Foreign Languages Press, Peking: Collet's, 1963. *Selected Works.* 5 vols. Lawrence & Wishart, 1954.

North, Robert, *Moscow and the Chinese Communists.* (2nd ed.) Stanford University Press, 1963.

Payne, Robert, *Portrait of a Revolutionary: Mao Tse-tung.* Abelard-Schuman, 1961.

Peck, Graham, *Two Kinds of Time*. Houghton Mifflin, 1950.

Schwartz, Benjamin, *Chinese Communism and the Rise of Mao*. Harvard University Press: Oxford University Press, 1951.

Siao-yu, *Mao Tse-tung and I Were Beggars*. Syracuse University Press, 1959.

Snow, Edgar, *Red Star Over China*. Gollancz, 1937.

Tang, Tsou, *America's Failure in China 1941-1950*. University of Chicago Press, 1963.

Valeo, Francis, *The China White Paper*. U.S. Library of Congress Legislative Reference Service, 1949.

CHAPTER 8: NATION UNDER COMMUNIST RULE

Alley, Rewi, *China's Hinterland in the Leap Forward*. New World Press, Peking, 1961.

Barnett, A. Doak, *China on the Eve of Communist Takeover*. Frederick A. Prae-ger, New York, 1963. *Communist China and Asia*. Vintage Books, New York, 1961.

Chen, Theodore H. E., *Thought Reform of the Chinese Intellectuals*. Hong Kong University Press, 1960.

Hughes, T. J., and Luard, D. E. T., *The Economic Development of Communist China, 1949-1958*. Oxford University Press, 1959.

Li, Choh-ming, *Economic Development of Communist China*. University of California Press, 1959.

MacFarquhar, Roderick, *The Hundred Flowers Campaign and the Chinese Intellectuals*. Atlantic Books, 1960.

Rostow, W. W., *et al.*, *The Prospects for Communist China*. Technology Press, Cambridge, Mass., 1954.

Snow, Edgar, *The Other Side of the River*. Gollancz, 1963.

Walker, Richard, *China under Communism*. Allen & Unwin, 1956.

CHAPTERS 9 AND 10: FOREIGN RELATIONS

Boorman, Howard L., Eckstein, Alexander, Mosely, Philip E., and Schwartz, Benjamin, *Moscow-Peking Axis, Strengths and Strains*. Harper & Brothers, New York, 1957.

Bowie, Robert R., and Fairbank, John K., *Communist China 1955-1959, Policy Documents with Analysis*. Harvard University Press, 1962.

Cheng Tien-fong, *A History of Sino-Russian Relations*. Public Affairs Press, Washington, 1957.

Dallin, David, *The Rise of Russia in Asia*. Hollis & Carter, 1950.

Fairbank, John K., *The United States and China*. (Rev. ed.) Harvard University Press, 1962.

Hudson, G. F., Lowenthal, Richard, and MacFarquhar, Roderick, *The Sino-Soviet Dispute*. Frederick A. Praeger, New York, 1961.

FAMOUS FIGURES AND WORKS IN CHINESE CULTURE

HISTORY AND LITERATURE

Anonymous	c.800-202 B.C.	Confucian Classics: *Book of Changes*; *Book of Documents*; *Book of Poetry*; *Book of Rites*; *Spring and Autumn Annals*. Tradition says Confucius compiled three of these books.
Ch'u Yuan	4th century B.C.	*Li Sao (On Encountering Sorrow)*, allegorical, rambling poem describing Ch'u Yuan's fruitless search for a worthy place for himself
Tso Ch'iu-ming	3rd century B.C.	*Tso Commentary*, detailed portrayal of aristocratic life in the 8th to 5th centuries B.C.
Ssu-ma Hsiang-ju	179-117 B.C.	*Tzu-hsu* and other essays written in poetry
Ssu-ma Ch'ien	149-90 B.C.	*Historical Records*, the first official history
Pan family	A.D. 3-116	*History of the Former Han Dynasty*, the first history of a single dynasty
Lu Chi	261-303	*Essay on Literature*, a description and analysis of the art of writing
Liu Hsieh	5th-6th century	*Literary Mind*, highly developed literary criticism discussing technique, style and function
Li Po	701-762	One of the greatest T'ang poets: "Night Thoughts", "The Song of Wine"
Tu Fu	712-770	One of China's greatest poets and the founder of the realistic school of poetry
Po Chu-i	772-846	Poet-official who served as Governor of Honan province: "The Everlasting Sorrow"
Ou-yang Hsiu	1007-1072	Leading Sung prose writer of philosophical and political treatises
Ssu-ma Kung	1019-1086	Author of a history of China from the 5th century B.C. to A.D. 959
Huang T'ing-chien	1045-1105	An innovator in extensive use of allusion and of the vernacular in poetry: *Collection of Worn-Out Brooms*
Kao Ch'i	1336-1374	An official who was probably the greatest of the Ming poets: *The Earthen Pot Resounds*
Wu Ch'eng-en	c.1500-1580	Satirical novel: *Record of a Journey to the West*
P'u Sung-ling	1640-1715	*Strange Stories*, a collection of 431 polished tales on supernatural themes
Hung Sheng	1650-1704	Drama: *The Immortal Palace*, the best of many treatments of the story of Emperor Ming Huang
Anonymous	17th century	*Chin P'ing Mei*, first Chinese novel of everyday life
Ts'ao Chan and Kao E	18th century	Novel: *Dream of the Red Chamber*
Wu Ching-tzu	1701-1754	Novel: *Unofficial History of Officialdom*
Liu E	1857-1909	*The Travels of Lao-ts'an*, a link between the traditional and the modern novel
Lu Hsun	1881-1936	Short stories and essays appraising China's domestic condition: *The True Story of Ah Q*
Hsu Chih-mo	1895-1931	First Chinese poet to use the modern vernacular successfully in poetry
Mao Tun	1896-	Government official. Novels: *The Eclipse*; *Rainbow*; *The Twilight*
Lao She	1898-	Novels: *The Philosophy of Old Chang*; *Rickshaw Boy*
Shen Ts'ung-wen	1902-	Short stories: "The Housewife". Novel: *The Long River*
Chiang Kuei	1908-	Novel: *The Whirlwind*
Ts'ao Yu	1910-	Plays: *The Thunderstorm*; *Sunrise*
Chien Chung-shu	c.1911-	Government official, literary critic and novelist. Satirical novel: *The Besieged City*
Eileen Chang	1920-	Satires of life under the Communists: *The Rice-Sprout Song*; *Love in Redland*

PHILOSOPHY AND POLITICAL THOUGHT

Lao Tzu	6th century B.C.	Traditional founder of philosophical Taoism. His thought is embodied in *Classic of the Way and the Power*, which probably dates from the 4th century B.C.
Confucius (K'ung Tzu)	551-479 B.C.	Founder of philosophy which emphasizes morality, duty and proper relationships between superiors and inferiors
Mo Ti (Mo Tzu)	c.470-391 B.C.	Anti-Confucianist who preached love, non-aggression and utilitarianism
Mencius (Meng Tzu)	c.372-289 B.C.	Disciple of Confucius who say man's innate goodness as the source of good government
Chuang Tzu	c.369-286 B.C.	Taoist mystic who glorified spiritual freedom in brilliant allegorical essays
Hsun Tzu	c.300-237 B.C.	Confucianist who regarded man's nature as evil but susceptible to change
Wei Yang	died 338 B.C.	Supposed author of *Book of Lord Shang*, a treatise expressing the Legalist belief that sound government is based on a system of "rewards and punishments"

Han Fei Tzu	died 233 B.C.	A Legalist. He advocated harsh totalitarian rule
Han Yu	A.D. 768-824	Founder of a Neo-Confucian movement that later flowered in the Sung Dynasty
Wang Yang-ming	1472-1528	Ming Dynasty Confucianist who saw man's mind as the centre of the universe
K'ang Yu-wei	1858-1927	Political reformer. He sought justification for modernization of China in the thesis that Confucius was an advocate of change: *Grand Unity*; *Confucius as a Reformer*
Sun Yat-sen	1866-1925	Father of the Chinese revolution. His philosophy is embodied in *San Min Chu I*, or "Three Principles of the People"
Ch'en Tu-hsiu	1879-1942	Scholar and founder of the influential magazine *New Youth*
Chiang Kai-shek	1887-	Analysis of China's history and contemporary problems: *China's Destiny*; *Soviet Russia in China*
Hu Shih	1891-1962	Historian and philosopher: *The Chinese Renaissance*
Mao Tse-tung	1893-	Essays: "On Contradiction"; "On New Democracy"; "On the Protracted War"

PAINTING

Anonymous	202 B.C.-A.D. 220	Wall paintings in palaces, portraits on silk, human figures on tiles
Anonymous	*c.*400-587	Buddhist wall paintings in Tun-huang caves
Ku K'ai-chih	344-406	*Admonitions to the Court Ladies* and other palace scenes, and *Nymph of the Lo River*
Chang Seng-yu	*c.*500-550	One of the first to paint somewhat fleshy figures: *Five Planets and Twenty-Eight Constellations*
Wang Wei	699-759	First to use "broken-ink" method
Chang Hsuan	*c.*750	*Ladies Preparing Newly Woven Silk*
Han Kan	*c.*750	Most famous painter of the prized horses that came to T'ang capitals from western Asia
Chou Fang	*c.*780-810	Known for his insight into a fleeting moment: *Barbarian Tribute Bearers*
Wu Tao-tzu	*c.*700-760	Demons, dragons and Buddhist saints on temple walls at Changan and Loyang
Yen Li-pen	640-680	Scholar-official. He painted portraits of scholars and famous men: *Thirteen Emperors*
Ching Hao and Kuan T'ung	906-960	Pioneers in the development of China's monumental landscape technique
Shih K'o	10th century	Vigorous and spontaneous painter of secular, Taoist and Buddhist subjects
Tung Yuan	10th century	Landscapes from the area just south of the Yangtze River
Chao Kan	10th century	*River Journey at Early Snowfall*
Li Ch'eng	940-990	Greatest of Chinese landscapists. He expressed a belief in the underlying coherence in nature
Kuo Hsi	*c.*1020-1090	Influential member of the Imperial Academy at Kaifeng. His work showed turbulence, fantasy and realism: *Early Spring*; *Autumn in the River Valley*
Li Lung-mien	*c.*1040-1106	*The Five Horses*; *Metamorphoses of the Heavenly Beings*
Ts'ui Po	11th century	Skill and spontaneity in animal subjects: *Hare Scolded by Jay*; *Bamboo and Heron*
Mi Fei	1051-1107	Poet, calligrapher, scholar-official. He developed the "ink-dot" style
Emperor Hui Tsung	12th century	Patron of the Imperial Academy. He himself painted flowers and birds
Li T'ang	Flourished *c.*1100-1130	"Painter-in-attendance" of the Hangchow Academy: *A Myriad Trees on Strange Peaks*
Liang K'ai	*c.*1140-1210	Buddhist subjects and landscapes: *Li Po Chanting a Poem*
Ma Yuan	*c.*1150-1230	*Walking on a Mountain Path in Spring*; *A Scholar and His Servant on a Terrace*
Hsia Kuei	*c.*1180-1230	*A Pure and Remote View of Rivers and Mountains*
Ma Lin	1190-1260	*Listening to the Wind in the Pines*; *The Fragrance of Spring Clearing after Rain*
Mu-ch'i	*c.*1220-1290	Buddhist subjects and landscapes: *Persimmons*; *Mother Monkey and Child*
Kao K'o-kung	*c.*1248-1310	Government official and landscapist: *Verdant Peaks above the Clouds*
Chao Meng-fu	1254-1322	Government official and scholar-painter: *Autumn Colours on the Ch'iao and Hua Mountains*
Huang Kung-wang	1269-1354	Landscapist with a deceptively simple style: *Dwelling in the Fu-ch'un Mountains*
Ni Tsan	1301-1374	Landscapist, renowned for the restraint of his style: *Trees in a River Valley at Yu-shan*
Wang Meng	*c.*1309-1385	An artist concerned with space and emotional expression: *Forest Dwellings at Chu-ch'u*
Sheng Mou	*c.*1310-1361	Landscapist whose work is notable for its delicate lines and touches of colour
Tai Chin	15th century	Founder of the Che School of landscape painting, characterized by swift, spontaneous, brilliant technique
Shen Chou	1427-1509	Poet and writer. He founded the Wu School which stressed balance and meditative qualities
Wu Wei	1459-1508	Ming court painter of Che School: *The Pleasures of the Fishing Village*; *Scholar Seated under a Tree*
T'ang Yin	1470-1524	*Clearing after Snow in a Mountain Pass*; *Secluded Fishermen on an Autumn River*
Wen Cheng-ming	1470-1559	Ming official. His landscapes were sombre and austere: *Old Trees by a Cold Waterfall*
Lu Chi	Flourished 1488-1505	Most famous bird and flower painter at Ming court: *Geese beside a Snowy Bank*
Lu Chih	1496-1576	Poet and calligrapher, painter of the Wu School: *Autumn Colours at Hsung-yang*; *River Scene in Spring*
Ch'iu Ying	*c.*1510-1551	A creator of fragile palace scenes and landscapes: *Spring Morning in the Han Palace*
Tung Ch'i-ch'ang	1555-1636	Official and connoisseur of painting and calligraphy. He classified 10 centuries of Chinese paintings and made many attributions of master paintings
Wang Shih-ming	1592-1680	Ming official. His work was known for the denseness and complexity of its brushwork
Ch'en Hung-shou	1599-1652	Landscapist and figure artist: *Boating on the Lake*
Shih-ch'i	*c.*1610-1693	Buddhist monk and artist. He used glowing light in *The Pao-en Temple*
Chu Ta	1625-*c.*1705	Painter of powerful, nervous landscapes and glowering birds and fish
Wang Yuan-ch'i	1642-1715	High government official and artist in charge of the imperial collection of painting and calligraphy
Ch'i Pai-shih	1863-1957	Traditional painter of flowers, insects and shellfish
Chang Ta-ch'ien	1899-	Landscapist and flower painter

Credits

Sources for the illustrations and certain translations are shown below. Credits for pictures from left to right are separated by commas, top to bottom by dashes.

Cover—Henri Cartier-Bresson from Magnum

8, 9—Der Stern from Black Star

12—Map by Rafael D. Palacios

14—Tao-Tai Hsia from *China's Language Reforms*, the Institute of Far Eastern Languages, Yale University Press, New Haven, 1956

18, 19—Henri Cartier-Bresson except top left, John Massey-Stewart

20, 21—Tom Hutchins, W. and B. Forman from *The Face of Ancient China*, Spring Books, London—Fernand Gignon

22, 23—Henri Cartier-Bresson from Magnum

24, 25—Claude Arthaud and François Hebert-Stevens

26—Dmitri Kessel

29, 30—Quote from Wu Wang: based on James Legge, *The Chinese Classics*, Vol. III, Hong Kong University Press, 1960

31—Map by Rafael D. Palacios

34—Der Stern from Black Star

35 to 39—Dmitri Kessel

40—M. Cyril from Black Star

42—Der Stern from Black Star

44—Quote from Ssu-ma Ch'ien: Burton Watson, *Records of the Grand Historian of China*, Columbia University Press

46—Quote from Han Yu: Edwin O. Reischauer, *Ennin's Travels in T'ang China*, Ronald Press

49 to 55—Dmitri Kessel

56, 57—Tom Hutchins—William Vandivert, Chuang Hseh-peng

58, 59—Henry B. Beville

61—Quote from Tsung Ping: *Source of Chinese Tradition*, compiled by William Theodore de Bary, Wing-tsit Chan, and Burton Watson, Columbia University Press

63—Drawings by Adolph E. Brotman

64—Quote from Tu Fu: William Hung, *Tu Fu, China's Greatest Poet*, Harvard University Press

66—Ann Rosener from Pix

67—Richard Meek

68 to 71—Henry B. Beville

72, 73—Robert Crandall

74, 75—Lynn St. John

76, 77—Der Stern from Black Star

80—Drawing by Matt Greene

84, 85—Dmitri Kessel, Ewing Krainin

86—Howard Sochurek—Der Stern from Black Star

87—Dmitri Kessel

88, 89—Claude Arthaud and François Hebert-Stevens

90—Rey Scott

93—Peabody Museum of Salem

99—Wide World Photos, Wu Chung Yee

100—European Picture Service—The Bettmann Archive

101—Bottom, United Press International

102, 103—Left, Earl Leaf from Rapho-Guillumette; centre, Bosshard from Black Star; right, Frontier Films

104—Jack Wilkes—Official Executive Headquarters Photo

105—George M. Lacks—Jack Birns

106, 107—James Burke

111—Map by Rafael D. Palacios

114—Eastfoto

115—Takayuki Senzaki

116 to 118—Harry Redl from Black Star

119—Bottom, Sankei Shimbum

120, 121—Der Stern from Black Star except bottom left, Caio Mario Garrubba from Rapho-Guillumette

122, 123—Caio Mario Garrubba from Rapho-Guillumette

130 to 134—Der Stern from Black Star

135 to 141—Henri Cartier-Bresson from Magnum

149—K. H. Chu

150, 151—Harry Redl from Black Star except left, Inger Abrahamsen from Rapho-Guillumette

152, 153—John Dominis except right, Inger Abrahamsen from Rapho-Guillumette

154, 155—John Dominis except top right, Horace Bristol

156, 157—John Dominis

158—John Dominis—Horace Bristol

159—John Dominis

160—Harry Redl from Black Star

165—W. and B. Forman from *The Face of Ancient China*, Spring Books, London

166, 167—Caio Mario Garrubba from Rapho-Guillumette

ACKNOWLEDGMENTS

The editors of this book are indebted to the following scholars, who read and commented on portions of the text: A. Doak Barnett, Chairman, Contemporary China Studies Committee, East Asian Institute, Columbia University; Howard L. Boorman, Director, Research Project on Men and Politics in Modern China, Columbia University; C. T. Hu, Professor of Education, Teachers College, Columbia University; and F. W. Mote, Professor of Oriental Studies, Princeton University. The author expresses his appreciation to Conrad Brandt, St. Antony's College, Oxford; Stanley Karnow; Sydney Liu; Charles Mohr; and Guy Searls.

Index

This symbol in front of a page number indicates a photograph or painting of the subject mentioned.

Finito di stampare nel mese di aprile 1968 presso le Officine Grafiche Arnoldo Mondadori - Verona - Printed in Italy